AUTHENTICATING APOSTOLICITY

Discerning True Apostles in an Age of Spiritual Ambition

Edwrin Sutton

Unless otherwise indicated, all scripture quotations are from the Holy Bible King James Version, which is in the public domain.

CONTENTS

ACKNOWLEDGMENTS

I gladly acknowledge my wife, Nakia, my right-hand person in every aspect of my life. I am a better man because of you.

I am very grateful for and to my mother, Dr. Valentine Sutton. Without your standards, I would not be where I am today.

To The Sending Church, thank you for serving alongside me. I am honored to be a part of such an impactful extension of the Kingdom of God.

To my pastor, Bishop Michael A. Blue, thank you so much for your profound wisdom, insight, and leadership. You are indeed an apostle.

FOREWORD

APOSTLES: A CONTROVERSIAL CONCEPT

Controversial. The Church, its Founder, its subsequent adherents, and its teachings have always been the seedbed for debate: "controversial." One example of a structural element of the Church to which the term "controversial" may be duly applied is the current, at times volatile, conversation regarding "apostles." Virtually no one contradicts the historical fact that Yeshua (Jesus) of Nazareth, a First Century Jewish Rabbi, had a cadre of inner circle followers that have come to be known to the world as "The Twelve," "The Twelve Disciples," or "The Twelve Apostles." However, the challenge arises when some suggest that there might be, or have been, others – even contemporary followers of that same Rabbi - who might appropriately bear the designation "apostle." Really? That is controversial.

Yes, the range of opinions is vast: from the extremely conservative view that The Twelve were the only Apostles ever, to an exaggeratedly liberal view that seems to imply that anyone who bestows the label upon himself / herself (or can find someone else willing to do the "bestowal") may rightly be called an apostle. By the way, the extreme conservatives say that even Matthias (who was selected through the prayers and casting of lots of The Eleven to replace Judas – Acts Chapter 1) was an illegitimate apostolic replacement. They declare that Matthias was man's choice, but not God's. Paul, they say, was the one whom God had foreordained to take Judas' slot among the other Apostles: there were only ever to have been Twelve.

The controversy is exacerbated by the fact that, throughout the two millennia of the Church's existence, there have periodically been individuals and groups who made apostolic claims. Some operated under the grand delusion that they were somehow the re-incarnation or the "new-and-improved version" of some Biblical character or status. Consequently, particularly in modern times, such delusions have had such an extremely damming effect - in many cases a well-deserved damnation - that even the thought of any ongoing connectivity today with any of the first century's spiritual ministry gifts ("apostle" is referred to as a "gift" in Ephesians 4:8,11), manifestations, or works of God are often viewed with high skepticism, both within and outside the Church.

For years up till the present, those who believe the divinely supernatural gifts no longer exist in the Church have been called "cessationists." In today's theological circles, those who believe in "ongoing connectivity" of first century divinely supernatural gifts of Christ are referred to as "continuationists". The position of this book and of its author falls between the two extremes, safely between the two – Scripturally, therefore safely.

The position of this book is continuationist, but not without sober qualification and stipulation. There are more details within the book but suffice it to say here that this writing has as its premise the affirmation that the Bible is the only divinely inspired, written revelation, the Word of God. The Bible has no peers: past, present, or future. Therefore, all insights or individuals subsequent to the Bible, from the first to the twenty-first centuries and beyond, are subordinate to the Bible: **none have equal authority to the Bible**, and all are subject to the Bible. Moreover, as The Twelve Apostles are all dead, including Matthias and Paul, this author asserts that no one alive today has the authoritative status that was granted to them and the other historically foundational members of Christ's Church, such as James and Jude. They have no peers.

With that said, this book also affirms the following:

1. God, by definition, is Spirit. Though He is the Author of nature, He is not limited to the natural: He transcends time, space, matter, and energy. He is Super-natural.

2. God, by definition, is omnipotent and revelatory.

3. God, in His omnipotence, has preserved one written revelation of Himself: The Bible.

4. God, by definition, is immutable: He never changes.

5. God, as self-revealed in the Bible, is not the detached Deity of "deism", the seventeenth century idea that God created and set the universe in motion, as a divine Clockmaker, but has no further interaction with His creation, having left it on "cruise-control" via the laws of nature.

6. God, as Self-revealed in the Bible, is clearly not deistic but dynamic: He interacts with His creatures ---- He speaks; He judges; He delivers; He heals; He saves.

7. The Bible's records of the **past** and revelations of the **future** - they **all** contain the interaction and intervention of the omnipotent, immutable God with His people.

   (Even the record of the Intertestamental Period – the time covered between the Books of Malachi and Matthew - bears witness to God being Personally active and interactive in the lives of His people.)

   Church History after the Bible is punctuated with divinely supernatural intervention.

8. Nowhere does The Bible teach that God has withdrawn His Hand now, in the reality of the **present.** The unchanging God has not morphed from **dynamic** in the past and thefuture **to deistic** for the **present.**

9. Though God's nature has not changed, His people can and do change. Bible history and Church history, including the Old

and New Testament eras and beyond, demonstrate that certain Biblical truths have at times been de-emphasized, denied, distorted, or diminished. For example, even a truth as fundamental to Christianity as justification by faith had to be "restored" to doctrinal centrality via the Protestant Reformation.

10. Even so, there have been other Biblical truths, not as central, yet vital for the wholesomeness of the Body of Christ and its witness to the world, that have needed "restoration," i.e., not the introduction of some esoteric doctrine, but the recovery of principles or practices that are thoroughly Biblically founded but neglected for various reasons.

11. The immutable God established the Church as He intended, at the expense of the precious Blood of the Lamb of God, Jesus Christ. His intention included an unchanging Foundation of which Jesus is the Chief Cornerstone. This unchanging Foundation includes those original Followers who taught Christ's teachings to their generations and caused them to be recorded for future generations.

12. However, through and upon the unchanging Foundation, God's intention **was and still is** the building of a living, ever-growing, maturing ORGANISM, called The Church.

"And are built upon the foundation of the apostles and prophets, Jesus Christ Himself being the Chief Cornerstone, in whom all the building fitly framed together groweth unto an holy temple in the Lord: In whom ye also are builded together for an habitation of God through the Spirit."
Ephesians 2:20-22

AN ILLUSTRATION: In the construction of a natural house in this region of the US, the foundation is typically comprised of concrete and bricks of the highest quality that the homeowner can afford, because the foundation is to be unmoved and immovable.

There can be no compromise in the foundation, for it is of primary significance to the entire edifice.

> However, often the rest of the home --- e.g., the walls, walkways, gateways, fences, porches --- may also be composed of bricks and / or concrete, with other complementary materials. This further extensive use of bricks in the residence's construction in no way diminishes the essentiality or uniqueness of the role of the bricks in their position within the home's foundation. To the contrary, for the rest of the structure to conform to the quality, stability, and durability of the foundation, it necessitates high quality materials throughout the edifice. Indeed, the utilization of such materials in the rest of the house increases the value of the house.

Even so, this book's position has nothing to do with re-constructing Christ's Church's Foundation or presuming to "improve" upon It. Instead, its emphasis is upon the ongoing ministry of the apostolic *within* the Church, as one leadership ministry stream among many in the present day. It clarifies the *foundational responsibility* of modern church leadership to ensure that we are true to what Christ declared He would build (Matthew 16:18), and that our efforts as His "sub-contractors" (I Corinthians 3:9) would conform to the methods and "materials list" set forth by our eternal Chief Architect and General Contractor (Hebrews 3:4,12:2) in His Blueprint, the Bible, which is the Word of God.

Thus, the author's reference to current apostles having a foundational function does not include the Foundational Role of the historic establishment of the Body of Christ and its orthodox doctrines: that has been done "once and for all." Rather, his usage is an analogical application of the term to each local congregation, region, or other sphere of influence / scope of work to which a servant of God may be called to initiate or engage.

The fact that there have been false apostles is no more a conclusive argument against the existence of genuine apostles than is the equally sad realization that there have been false pastors and teachers a total negation of the authentic ministry of true shepherds in the

House of God. We should expect that all of Christ's gifts (Ephesians 4:11), despite Satan's counterfeits, will thrive in the Church "till we all come..."

"Till we all come in the unity of the faith, and of the knowledge of the Son of God, unto a perfect man, unto the measure of the stature of the fulness of Christ..."
Ephesians 4:13

Yet, Scripture admonishes us to examine ourselves and to take heed as to how we build upon God's foundation. Moreover, Christ directs us to scrutinize "fruit" in order to identify His true followers.

"For we are laborers together with God: ye are God's husbandry, ye are God's building. According to the grace of God which is given unto me, as a wise master builder, I have laid the foundation, and another buildeththereon. But let every man take heed how he buildeth thereupon. For other foundation can no man lay than that is laid, which is Jesus Christ."
I Corinthians 3:9-11

"Beware of false prophets, which come to you in sheep's clothing, but inwardly they are ravening wolves. Ye shall know them by their fruits. Do men gather grapes of thorns, or figs of thistles? Even so every good tree bringeth forth good fruit; but a corrupt tree bringeth forth evil fruit...Wherefore by their fruits ye shall know them."
(Matthew 7:15-17, 20)

Therefore, **Pastor Edwrin Sutton** is purposeful in presenting this new volume, *Authenticating Apostolicity.* He intentionally equips us by highlighting scripturally prescribed tools for these leaders' *self-examination* (personally and ministerially) and providing the Bible's criteria by which believers may exercise discernment, to *"know them* *that labor among us*" (I Thessalonians 5:12-14). **Pastor Sutton** faces the apostolic controversy courageously. He challenges us with a provocative perspective as to how God's active work through the grace of the apostolic is still beneficially relevant to us all. In accepting this challenge, may we all be empowered to undergird more effectively *"the perfecting of the saints, for the work of the ministry, for the edifying of the Body of Christ."*

Bishop Michael A. Blue

Door of Hope Christian Church

Christian Covenant Fellowship of Ministries

Marion, South Carolina

CHAPTER
01
WHY SO MANY?

We are in a pandemic! This pandemic has nothing to do with COVID-19 or influenza. The Body of Christ is faced with a pandemic of so-called apostles.

Everywhere you turn, you meet "apostle so and so." It has become quite common in church circles. The question is, are there truly modern-day apostles? If there are any, certainly there cannot be this many.

AN APOSTOLIC SHIFT

When we look at the early church in the Book of Acts, each ascension gift was prominently on display. The didactic gift called *teacher* was already operating in the church at Antioch in Acts 13. And by the time Paul wrote to the church at Ephesus, the Church had all ascension gift offices fully functioning—apostles, prophets, teachers, evangelists, and pastors as laid out in Ephesians 4.

In the early church, the terms *pastor*, *bishop*, and *elder* were used interchangeably to denote an overseer[1]. By the end of the second century, however, the title of the Old Covenant office of *priest* introduced by the church in Rome had crept into the Church, hijacking the office of pastor/bishop. However, during the Protestant Reformation, the acknowledgment of the office of pastor was reinstated by a distinguished reformer, John Calvin[2]. It was at this time that the office of pastor grew in emphasis.

Then, during the era of the Great Awakening, we experienced an evangelistic shift. During the First Great Awakening, evangelists such as Jonathan Edwards, George Whitefield, Gilbert Tennent, and others were used mightily evangelistically. In the Second Great Awakening, Charles Finney and Dwight Moody (to name a couple) were used of God to bring thousands to the salvific (saving) knowledge of Christ.

In the tradition of Charles Finney and Dwight Moody, we came to the twentieth century with two bold Billys. Billy Sunday and Billy

Graham impacted the world evangelistically through coliseums, arenas, and mainstream television.

Again, all the gifts of God were present in the Church, but in the twentieth century, we experienced a more prominent shift toward the prophetic. Modern-day prophets of God were being raised up—I mean, true prophets of God. However, whenever something authentic from the Lord manifests, Satan always sends counterfeits. This began to take place in the mid-1900s. God used prophets such as William Branham, A. W. Tozer, and others mightily to foretell and forth-tell His oracles under the inspiration of the Spirit of God.

Now in the twenty-first century, there has indeed been a discernible shift toward the apostolic. We are in what I call *the new apostolic era*. Some have said that there has been a restoration of the office of apostle. However, the semantics of this statement are questionable. The truth is, all of the gifts of the Spirit have been in operation since the day of Pentecost in the Book of Acts. However, over time, we have lost the acknowledgment of all the gifts.

That said, with this new apostolic era, there is also a new apostolic error. Some individuals discern the turn but do not understand the meaning of the turn. You see, whenever we do not understand something but merely sense it, we are more prone to error if we do not seek clarity. It would seem that the Body (of Christ) has shifted, but now the joints of the Body have been dislocated. Let us use the analogy of the physical body to show how a dislocation takes place. When a strong impact happens to a physical body, bones often slip out of a joint. This is called a dislocation.

With the Church, whenever the Body experiences a shift—a new impact—it can cause the joints to become dislocated. What we are witnessing in our day is dislocation among the joints of the Body. While we have experienced an apostolic shift within the Body of Christ as a whole, many of the joints of the Body have shifted out of place. Although by right the entire Body should be apostolic, not every joint of the Body is an apostle.

Experts say that if you dislocate one of your joints, you should treat it as an emergency. It saddens me that in the case of the Church, our joints have been dislocated, but we are not treating it as an emergency. Ephesians 4:16 informs us that every joint of the Body of Christ is to supply strength to the Body. However, when the joint is out of place, it cannot provide the strength the Body needs. We as a whole are void of strength because we are suffering from an identity crisis within the Body.

How is this so? When you identify as something that God has never called you to be, it is a sign that you are a dislocated joint.

What might be the causes of such an aberration?

Ignorance

The key reason so many individuals falsely call themselves *apostles* is their own ignorance. To be called ignorant is not derogatory or demeaning; it simply means "lacking in knowledge." Apparently, we are in tune with the turn, but we do not understand the terms of the turn. Many are calling themselves *apostles* because they do not understand the meaning of the term *apostle* in the context in which Jesus used it. And whenever you do not understand the context of a word, you have no clarity when it comes to its true meaning. Many of our brothers and sisters use the term *apostle* inappropriately because they do not truly understand its real meaning.

Lust for Power

Another reason why some call themselves apostles when they are not is that they want power. Anyone who lusts for power is a dangerous individual. Many might view the apostle as a big shot—one who is perceived as the most anointed, or the one who is in control. These are false perspectives regarding apostles. When you lust for power and have a skewed view of apostleship, you will claim a legitimate office illegitimately. The power-hungry seek titles for selfish motives.

Maybe they believe that claiming apostleship will grant them more money. Possibly, it will warrant absolute submission from those under their charge. But in the case of true apostles, the opposite is true. True apostles do not desire to gain more authority; it is others they desire to empower with more authority.

Desire to Be Significant

Lastly, some erroneously claim to be apostles because of an excessive desire for significance. It is true that everyone desires and needs to feel significant. As my pastor, Bishop Michael A. Blue, says, "Existence demands significance." Everything that God created is an answer to a problem. Therefore, your existence is proof of your significance.

However, some have an unhealthy desire for significance. Oftentimes, the false claim of apostleship is because they want to be seen, feared, or revered as greatly anointed. So, in order for me to have significant respect, I will claim to be an apostle. To prohibit individuals from treating me and perceiving me as inferior, I will label myself as an apostle. For the purpose of convincing people to tithe to me, I will claim to be an apostle. Since I want to sit on a throne (*insert laugh*), I will therefore go by the honorific *apostle*.

Friends, how saddening this truly is. If you believe that a title is the magic garment that suddenly clothes you with importance, then what you need is not another ceremony, another ordination service, or another chain draped around your neck—you need a hug, a faithful friend who will speak truth to you, and some unhurried, life-transforming time in the presence of Jesus. Without Him, titles are just words stitched on empty garments.

Most of the problems we see plaguing the modern Church—particularly within many predominantly Black congregations in the West—stem from this deep, misplaced lust for titles, positions, and recognition. And while the surface looks like simple pride or ambition, beneath it may lie something more complex and tragic: a wound passed down through generations.

The African American experience in the West is deeply marked by centuries of oppression, systemic injustice, and dehumanization. For hundreds of years, our people were told they were property, not persons; inferior, not equal; laborers, not leaders. Such relentless oppression has a way of scarring the self-image of an individual—and indeed of an entire people group. When your ancestors were stripped of name, voice, and dignity, the hunger to be seen and acknowledged can run deep, even if it sometimes seeks expression in unhealthy ways.

In that light, the lust for titles can be more than ego—it can be an attempt to reclaim significance, to prove worth, to declare, "I am somebody!" Yet when that search for validation is not rooted in Christ, it becomes a fragile substitute, a hollow crown that cannot truly heal the wound.

And again, how saddening this is. Because in God's Kingdom, true significance is not earned through a title—it is received through adoption. Your worth was settled at the cross. No earthly office can increase it, and no absence of office can diminish it. The title may impress people for a moment, but intimacy with Jesus will shape you for eternity.

Titles do not make you more attractive to the economy of heaven. Nevertheless, titles do make you more attractive to the economy of hell. Proceed with caution!

The Imposture: A Tactic of Satan

No matter what the individual reason is for false apostles to make such a claim, it is ultimately Satan's ploy to cause confusion. Why does this even matter? Why not allow people to be comfortable claiming to be something that they are not if it makes them happy?

Whenever you make an illegitimate claim to something that is legitimate, you are actually being used strategically by Satan, whether you know it or not. For example, a young lady who has encountered abusive, unfaithful, and disrespectful men has a greater tendency to generalize that "all men are dogs." When you see and hear in the media repetitively of preachers caught in immoral acts, you are more prone not to trust anyone who claims to be a preacher. Satan knows this. He should because he is the originator of deception. 2 Corinthians 11:14 declares that Satan masquerades as an angel of light. The impostor wolf in sheep's clothing is him. So, if I introduce you to a pack of wolves in sheepskin, you may never trust an authentic sheep again.

This applies to the massively false claim of apostleship as well. When you encounter a disproportionate number of so-called apostles who are not, it further helps cessationists (that is, people who say that gone are the days of the prophets and apostles) to refute belief in modern-day apostles. Moreover, it becomes a further stumbling block for others to receive from those who truly are. When you falsely claim to be an apostle, you provoke others to disgrace the grace.

It is my prayer that after having read this book, those who have either ignorantly or arrogantly made the faulty claim of apostleship would have such a strong conviction that they would repent. We do not want to cooperate with Satan by being used as a vehicle of deception to prevent others from growing in the knowledge of God.

At the same time, this book does not cover everything to do with the apostolic. We will not be talking about apostolic measure, apostolic scope, and so forth. This book is solely to teach us what an apostle is and what an apostle is not, so that we are equipped to identify the real deal. There are so many truths regarding apostles that will not be shared in this book. I know in part and am still learning and growing in the things of God.

I have also been intentional about staying away from my personal opinions regarding apostles that cannot be consistently affirmed by the scriptures. However, I do believe that as you make this journey with me, you will be inspired and possibly more informed about the main things related to apostolic DNA.

So, join me on this daring trip of authenticating apostolicity. We will delve into many erroneous claims of apostleship based on the working definition of apostle I offer. We will then look at the characteristics and markers of true "ascension gift" apostles based on biblical and historical exemplars, and finally arrive at objective criteria I propose to determine who accurately identifies as an apostle in our present era.

CHAPTER

02

MODERN-DAY APOSTLES?

F or as long as I can remember, I have been in a local church. I was raised in the Baptist Church from birth, and around the age of eleven, I transitioned to the Methodist Church. Although I admit I have not always been a fully committed believer, I have always had a heart for the Lord and a strong zeal for the things of God.

I started preaching the gospel "officially" at the age of nineteen. During those fledgling years of ministry, I glorified intellect over spirit. I did not believe in personal prophecy or contemporary prophets. I did not trust the Pentecostal Church because I thought it was devoid of intellect and sound doctrine.

But at the age of twenty-five, something dramatic happened that forced me to remove myself from some of the people I deeply loved. This separation brought about great pain and persecution for me. During those challenging days, I would be cooped up in my bedroom for days, crying and talking to the Lord. It was in that room, in that season of sorrow and solitude, that God did something powerfully new in me. Certain spiritual gifts that were dormant began to be stirred and awakened in me. Two of the gifts that really began to surface were the gift of prophecy and the word of knowledge.

I could write an entire chapter about how the Lord has used me in the prophetic. However, that is not the purpose of this book. I have shared all of that to say I understand why many of us do not believe in modern-day apostles. I was just like you. My narrow intellectual view of the Scriptures and Christ brought me to that conclusion. Nevertheless, despite what our private thoughts are, apostles still exist!

But as I have mentioned, cessationists believe that apostles ceased to exist sometime in the first century. One of the primary Scriptures that this school of thought uses is Ephesians 2:19-20:

> *Now therefore ye are no more strangers and foreigners, but fellowcitizens with the saints, and of the household of God; And are* **built upon the foundation of the apostles** *and prophets,* **Jesus Christ Himself being the chief cornerstone;**
> **—Ephesians 2:19-20**

This is one of their main Scriptures to support their claim. They say that since the Scriptures declare that the Church is built upon the foundation of the apostles and prophets, then there is no need for apostles and prophets anymore, since the foundation has already been laid. Let us unpack this further. If the foundation has already been laid and we therefore do not need apostles, we must go on to say that the cornerstone (Jesus Christ) has already been laid and therefore He is no longer needed or relevant to our lives.

How ludicrous. If we still need Jesus, although the *Chief Cornerstone* has already been laid, we still need apostles, although the foundation has already been laid.

Consider the foundation of a building. Foundations can be weakened through external forces like bombs and earthquakes, and also internal forces like mold, which causes rot and decay. The foundations of the Church throughout its history have been weakened more by internal forces. Some of these forces are false doctrines, heresies, and movements that contaminate the purity of the gospel. This started happening even in the days of the early church, when the apostle Paul warned the Church against wolves from within that would attempt to destroy the flock.

If even in those days the apostles were needed, how much more so now, when all sorts of false doctrines and teachings are rife within the Body of Christ. It would take the firm hand of those with apostolic authority to steer the Church back to its biblical foundations and rebuild the foundations that have rotted or decayed.

Although Ephesians 2:19-20 is a key text cessationists use, the most frequently used is 1 Corinthians 13:8-10, where Paul states that "prophecies will pass away, tongues will cease, knowledge will pass away." Many cessationists interpret "when that which is perfect comes" (v.10) as a reference to the completion of the New Testament Canon or the end of the apostolic era, thereby concluding that such gifts are no longer operative. However, this misinterpretation does not align with the textual, contextual, and theological trajectory of the New Testament and the early church. Rather, Paul anticipates the continuation of spiritual gifts until the eschaton (end of this age).

THE CESSATIONIST INTERPRETATION

Cessationists such as B. B. Warfield[3] and John MacArthur[4] have traditionally maintained that revelatory gifts were necessary for the foundational period of the Church and ceased once Scripture was complete. The key assumption in this interpretation is that "perfect" (*téleios*) refers to the completed canon. According to this reading, prophecy, tongues, and revelatory knowledge were only intended to support the early church until it reached doctrinal maturity through the inspired apostolic writings.

However, this interpretation imposes a later theological development onto the text and fails to consider the internal logic and surrounding literary context of 1 Corinthians 13.

My arguments:

1. Lexical and Contextual Analysis of *Teleios*

The Greek word *teleios* (τέλειον), translated as "perfect," can mean "complete," "mature," or "fully developed." In its New Testament usage, it often denotes moral or eschatological completeness (cf. Matt. 5:48; James 1:4; Phil. 3:12). There is no explicit indication in the immediate context that Paul refers to the canon of Scripture, a concept that was foreign to the Corinthian audience.

Moreover, in verse 12, Paul writes, "For now we see through a glass, darkly; but then face-to-face." The phrase "face-to-face" (*prosōpon pros prosōpon*) strongly echoes Old Testament language used to describe encounters with God (e.g., Exodus 33:11). Similarly, "but then shall I know even as also I am known" (v.12) parallels eschatological knowledge, not scholarly or doctrinal maturity (cf. 1 John 3:2). Thus, *teleios* most likely refers to the eschatological consummation at the return of Christ, not the closing of the canon.

2. Pauline Ecclesiology and the Function of Gifts

Paul consistently treats the gifts of the Spirit as ongoing mechanisms for building up the Church. In Ephesians 4:11-13, he states:

"And he gave some apostles; and some, prophets; and some, evangelists; and some, pastors and teachers; For the perfecting of the saints, for the work of ministry . . . Till we all come in the unity of the faith, and of the knowledge of the Son of God, unto a perfect man (*teleios anēr*)."

Here, Paul uses the same root word (*teleios*) to describe the Church's future maturity, reinforcing an eschatological goal. The preposition "till" (*mechri*) indicates that these gifts/offices, including apostles and prophets, are necessary until Christ's Body reaches final unity and maturity. This has clearly not yet occurred in full, suggesting that these roles have not expired. We will elaborate on this later.

Additionally, 1 Thessalonians 5:19-21 exhorts believers not to "despise prophecies," but to "test everything," providing no hint that the prophetic gift was temporary. The assumption throughout the New Testament is that spiritual gifts persist and are to be exercised with discernment.

3. Historical Evidence from the Early Church

Church history further undermines the cessationist view. Numerous early church fathers affirm the continued presence of spiritual gifts well into the second and third centuries:

- Irenaeus[5] (c. 180 AD), in *Against Heresies*, writes:

  "We do also hear many brethren in the Church who possess prophetic gifts, and who through the Spirit speak all kinds of languages" (Against Heresies, Book 5, Ch. 6.1).

- Tertullian[6] (c. 200 AD), a lawyer and theologian, affirmed the continuation of prophecy and described charismatic experiences in "On the Soul and Against Marcion."

- The Didache[7] (late first or early second century), an early church manual, contains explicit instructions on how to recognize and respond to itinerant prophets. This presupposes that prophecy was still widespread and authoritative in the post-apostolic church.

This early post-New Testament evidence demonstrates that the first generations of Christians did not believe the gifts had ceased with the death of the apostles or the writing of Scripture.

4. Theological and Scholarly Support for Continuationism

Modern scholarship increasingly challenges cessationist readings of 1 Corinthians 13. Notably:

- Gordon D. Fee[8], in his *God's Empowering Presence*, states:

  "There is not a single text in the New Testament that speaks of the cessation of the charismata before the parousia."

- Craig S. Keener[9], in *Gift and Giver*, writes:

  "Cessationism lacks any strong exegetical foundation and is primarily a post-biblical theological construct developed in reaction to abuse or perceived overemphasis on the charismatic gifts."

- Sam Storms[10], in *The Beginner's Guide to Spiritual Gifts*, offers extensive exegetical and theological arguments for the contemporary operation of all New Testament gifts.

These voices represent a growing scholarly consensus that the cessationist interpretation of 1 Corinthians 13:8-10 is exegetically weak and historically unfounded.

In conclusion, a careful exegesis of 1 Corinthians 13:8-10, when considered in the context of Pauline theology and early church history, reveals that the cessationist view rests on a misinterpretation of *teleios*. Paul clearly envisions an eschatological fulfillment that has not yet occurred—namely, the return of Christ and the final perfection of the Church. Until then, the gifts of the Spirit, including prophecy and apostolic leadership (in the non-canonical sense), remain vital for the edification, unity, and mission of the Church. Therefore, rather than arguing for the cessation of these gifts, the text calls for their responsible and Spirit-led exercise until Christ returns.

THE FIVE CLASSES OF APOSTLES

Now, oftentimes, individuals who are against the concept of modern-day apostles do not realize scripturally that there are five classes of apostles. The late Reverend Kenneth Hagin identifies four classes of apostles in *He Gave Gifts Unto Men.*[11]

The first class or category of apostle is:

1. Christ

Wherefore, holy brethren, partakers of the heavenly calling, consider **the Apostle** *and High Priest* **of our profession, Christ Jesus** *. . .*
—**Hebrews 3:1**

The Bible states that Jesus is an apostle. Jesus is not only an apostle; He is THE Apostle. He is the quintessential apostle. There will never be an apostle like Jesus. There will never be an exemplar outside of Jesus. Jesus is in a class all by Himself. This is a class of its own!

2. The Twelve Apostles of the Lamb

Wherefore of these men which have **companied with us all the time** *that the Lord Jesus went in and out among us,* **Beginning from the** **baptism of John, unto that same day that he was taken up from us,** **must one be ordained to be a witness with us of his resurrection.** *And they appointed two, Joseph called Barsabas, who was surnamed Justus, and Matthias. And they prayed, and said, Thou, Lord, which knowest the hearts of all men, shew whether of these two thou hast chosen, That he may take part of this ministry and apostleship, from which Judas by transgression fell, that he might go to his own place.* **And they gave forth their lots; and the lot fell upon Matthias; and he** **was numbered with the eleven apostles.**
—**Acts 1:21-26**

The second class is called *The Twelve Apostles of the Lamb*. This was a distinct class of apostles, which had one qualification with two distinct markers. The only qualification was that they had to have been with Jesus the entire time. The two markers that went with this were: they must have been around to witness Jesus's baptism and must have witnessed Jesus's ascension to heaven after His resurrection.

Now, there is no one living who qualifies to be a part of this class of apostle, not even the apostle Paul. We can say this is a closed class and has its own distinctives.

3. New Testament Scripture Writers

The third class of apostles are those who were New Testament Scripture writers. Apart from the writers among them who were second and third class apostles, such as John, Matthew, and Paul, there were also writers such as Mark, Luke, and Jude, who would also be considered apostles. This is because Scripture is foundational to our faith. Apostles are foundation layers and foundation reformers. From this time on, there will not be any more writers of Scripture.

4. The Ascension Gift Apostle

---

*But unto every one of us is given grace according to the measure of the gift of Christ. Wherefore he saith, **When he ascended up on high, he led captivity captive, and gave gifts unto men.** (Now that he ascended, what is it but that he also descended first into the lower parts of the earth? He that descended is the same also that ascended up far above all heavens, that he might fill all things. **And he gave some, apostles**; and some, prophets; and some, evangelists; and some, pastors and teachers . . .*
—Ephesians 4:7-11

The fourth class of apostle is *The Ascension Gift Apostle*. This is the category of apostle that this book attempts to discuss and authenticate. When Christ ascended into heaven and sent the promise of the Holy Spirit, He gave gifts. One of the gifts that He gave was the gift called *apostle*. If the ascension gift apostle is no longer active, as some suggest, then the ascension gifts prophet, evangelist, pastor, and teacher are no longer active either.

Let us look at a few ascension gift apostles in the Bible. As we noted, the "Twelve Apostles of the Lamb" who were eyewitnesses to Jesus are a closed class. But there are others in Scripture that were indeed apostles, namely:

- **Paul, Timothy, and Silvanus (Silas)**

Paul, and Silvanus, and Timotheus, unto the church of the Thessalonians which is in God the Father and in the Lord Jesus Christ: Grace be unto you, and peace, from God our Father, and the Lord Jesus Christ.
—1 Thessalonians 1:1

Notice that this letter is from Paul, Silas, and Timothy. Now read what Paul calls all three of them in chapter 2.

---

*For neither at any time used **we** flattering words, as ye know, nor a cloke of covetousness; God is witness: Nor of men sought **we** glory, neither of you, nor yet of others, when **we might have been burdensome, as the apostles of Christ**. But **we** were gentle among you, even as a nurse cherisheth her children: So being affectionately desirous of you, **we** were willing to have imparted unto you, not the gospel of God only, but also our own souls, because ye were dear unto us.*
—1 Thessalonians 2:5-8

Paul calls all three apostles of Christ.

- **James, the brother of Christ (not James from among the twelve)**

But other of the apostles saw I none, save James the Lord's brother.
—Galatians 1:19

- Apollos

---

*And these things, brethren, I have in a figure transferred to **myself
and to Apollos** for your sakes; that ye might **learn in us** not to think
of men above that which is written, that no one of you be puffed up
for one against another. For who maketh thee to differ from another?
and what hast thou that thou didst not receive? now if thou didst
receive it, why dost thou glory, as if thou hadst not received it? Now
ye are full, now ye are rich, ye have reigned as kings **without us**: and
I would to God ye did reign, that we also might reign with you. For I
think that God hath set forth **us the apostles** last, as it were appointed
to death: for **we** are made a spectacle unto the world, and to angels,
and to men.*
— 1 Corinthians 4:6-9

Paul calls Apollos and himself apostles.

- **Barnabas**

Which when the apostles, Barnabas and Paul, *heard of, they rent
their clothes, and ran in among the people, crying out . . .*
— Acts 14:14

Luke calls both Barnabas and Paul apostles.

- **Andronicus and Junia**

---

*Salute Andronicus and Junia, my kinsmen, and my fellow-prisoners,
who are of note among the apostles, who also were in Christ before me.*
—Romans 16:7

This passage of Scripture has been up for great debate. There are
two areas of controversy. The first school of thought believes that
Paul is identifying Andronicus and Junia as well-known apostles. The second school of thought believes that the text alludes to
Andronicus and Junia simply being well known by the apostles. I

cannot tell you with conviction which perspective is true. However, I believe that it is worth our consideration.

The point is, we must pay attention to the fact that the Scriptures show us that there were more than just the original twelve apostles. We have Jesus, the Twelve, Paul, Timothy, Silvanus a.k.a. Silas, James the brother of Jesus, Apollos, and Barnabas. Just those names alone make up nineteen apostles. If you consider Judas Iscariot, as well as Andronicus and Junia, that would be twenty-two apostles that the Scriptures call by name.

If we do not understand scripturally that there were more than twelve apostles throughout Scripture, we will not lay hold of current truths concerning the Kingdom of God.

5. Individuals in Apostolic Roles

This fifth class of apostle was revealed to Bishop Michael Blue. Individuals who serve in apostolic roles are a type of apostle, although they might not necessarily be in the category of ascension gift apostle. Individuals who serve as presiding prelates and legitimate bishops (special emphasis on legitimate) are serving in an apostolic capacity. Although some may not be ascension gift apostles, we should not have a problem with seeing presiding bishops as such. Why? Well, we do not have a problem calling a person a pastor, although they might not be an ascension gift pastor. We have no problem doing so because they are serving in a pastoral capacity. They might not be as patient and gentle as a fivefold gift pastor would be, but because they lead a congregation, we deem them as pastors.

Again, this does not mean that Presiding Prelate Applejack is a true ascension gift, an Ephesians 4:11 apostle. What this does mean is that Presiding Prelate Applejack is *their* (the fellowship's, the network's, or denomination's) apostle.

APOSTOLIC EXTINCTION

As shared, there are some who say that there is no longer any need for apostles. As a consequence, apostles no longer exist. Well, let us again consider Ephesians 4:11-13:

> *And he gave some, apostles; and some, prophets; and some, evangelists; and some, pastors and teachers; For the perfecting of the saints, for the work of the ministry, for the edifying of the body of Christ: Till we all come in the unity of the faith, and of the knowledge of the Son of God, unto a perfect man, unto the measure of the stature of the fulness of Christ . . .*

The Scriptures declare that the purpose of the apostle, prophet, evangelist, pastor, and teacher is 1) to equip the saints to do the work of ministry, and 2) to help mature (edify) the Body of Christ. This is the collective purpose of the fivefold ministry or, rather, ascension gifts.

For how long does the Bible declare that we will need these gifts?

1. **Until the Body of Christ is united.** The Church has come into The Faith, but we have not yet come into the unity of The Faith. Christ's Body is still very much divided. Just look at what members of the Body post on social media about other members of the Body. Look at our community pastors. By and large, we are isolated and separated from each other. If the Body of Christ is still divided, the scriptures declare that we still need all ascension gifts.

    Moreover, the Scripture stresses the unity of The Faith and the knowledge of the Son of God. We will always need the fivefold ministry until we all hold the same doctrinal truths, convictions, and devoted relationship (knowledge) with Christ. Do you remember what Christ prayed in the garden? His prayer was, *"Father, make them one . . ."* There will be a day when the Body of Christ will be one in every aspect of doctrine and devotion. Until then, we still need all the ascension gifts.

2. **Until the Body of Christ is full-grown.** The ascension gifts help to mature the Body. The perfect man in this passage is the fully mature man. A mature man is much stronger than a child. A mature man is an integrated whole. If the Body of Christ is still childish, not strong in charisma (power and gifts of the Spirit), and not strong in character (integrity and fruit of the Spirit), then we still need all fivefold gifts. Let me say it this way. If the three-year-old Body of Christ does not look like the full measure of the thirty-three-year-old Body of Christ, then all ascension gifts are still needed on the earth.

Let us also consider Romans 11:29: *"For the gifts and calling of God are without repentance."*

This is a text that is often misquoted and subsequently misinterpreted. Many will say, *"The gifts of God come without repentance."* The scriptures do not say that they *"come without repentance"* but rather that the gifts and callings *"are without repentance."* What this means is that God does not repent or regret giving you a gift or a calling. God does not change His mind about what He gave you. Praise God! If the gift of apostle is extinct, it would mean that God's Word is not true. According to Scripture, God's gifts are irrevocable. Therefore, the gift of apostle is irrevocable and is still alive on the earth.

Let us also consider Revelation 2:1-2.

*Unto the angel of the church of Ephesus write; These things saith he that holdeth the seven stars in his right hand, who walketh in the midst of the seven golden candlesticks; I know thy works, and thy labour, and thy patience, and how thou canst not bear them which are evil: **and thou hast tried them which say they are apostles, and are not, and hast found them liars** . . .*
—**Revelation 2:1-2**

Christ's chastisement of the church of Ephesus was balanced with His approval of how they examined those who claimed to be apostles. If Christ was pleased with how the church of Ephesus examined those who claimed to be apostles, surely He would be pleased if the modern-day Church were equally rigorous. This book matters. Authenticating apostolicity matters. The inspection of those who claim to be apostles matters.

However, if it was God's idea that there would not be any more apostles apart from the original twelve or thirteen, then the church at Ephesus would have had no need to test those who claimed to be apostles. Think about it. If there were no more apostles, it would not be necessary for this church to test those who claimed to be apostles. However, this church found it necessary to test professed apostles because, obviously, there were some true apostles and some false apostles. There was no need to test someone's apostolicity if there were no more apostles to test. In this case, all the individuals they encountered who claimed they were apostles did not pass their vetting. These individuals were lying.

It is also worth noting that in the New Testament, the word *pastors* is used only once. However, the word *apostle* or *apostles* is used seventy-eight times. It is ironic that today's Church highlights the pastor but sees no need for the apostle. The senior visionaries and senior overseers of the early church, which were birthed in the Book of Acts, were the apostles. Currently, the senior visionaries and senior overseers of the Church, by and large, are the pastors. This was never the design of God. Thank God for the advancement of our knowledge.

We build upon that which the apostles and prophets have laid. However, when the strong foundation that once was laid has been uprooted or weakened, it takes modern-day apostles to restore the foundations of truth. If we are called to edify and build up the Body of Christ, we must make sure that the foundation is solidified. Furthermore, if you are going to make the claim that apostles are no longer needed, you must also make the claim that the pastor is no longer needed, since they are both categorized as ascension gifts together.

CONCLUSION

Apostles still exist. Sometimes individuals dispute things they do not fully understand. However, with a thorough and sound panoramic view of Scripture, it is evident that the office of the apostle still remains.

In the next chapter, I will point out some of the erroneous claims to apostleship and talk about the main characteristics of an apostle.

CHAPTER
03
APOSTOLIC MYTHS

Before we define what an apostle actually is from a historic and scriptural standpoint, I want to set out a few myths regarding apostles. There are many absurd ideas that have surfaced regarding apostles and apostolic ministry. This chapter will help us address those ideas and help us transition into a weightier discussion regarding the demarcation of apostles.

MYTH #1

Planting a Church Makes an Individual an Apostle.

Just because someone has planted a church, or even churches, that does not officially make them an apostle. Church planting is absolutely one apostolic fruit, but not necessarily apostolic confirmation.

MYTH #2

Apostles Are Only Accountable to God.

Many so-called apostles claim that the only spiritual accountability they need is to God. How is this even biblical? Everyone needs human accountability. You are not being accountable to God if you are not accountable to the people God places around you. Human authority comes from God.

Some of us who claim to be Kingdom-minded do not faithfully attend a local assembly because of hurt, dissatisfaction, or maybe even prideful rebellion. I hate to say it, but you are not in the will of God. Let me explain.

If we claim to be in the Kingdom of God, please know that all kingdoms consist of a king, a constitution, and a military. This is by no means all that a kingdom consists of; however, this is all that we are highlighting at the moment.

Remember that which constitutes a kingdom. The King commands us through His law found in His constitution (the Bible) that we should not forsake the assembling of ourselves as some do. We also discover in the King's Constitution that at least once a week (on the sabbath), the King (Jesus) would go into the synagogue, and the Constitution says, "*as His custom was.*"

You want to be like Jesus? If so, go to the local assembly faithfully. I am not saying that you must remain in systems of abuse and religiosity. However, I am asking you to consider that the synagogue that Jesus faithfully attended was a place where He encountered many people who frequently attacked Him and who were thoroughly religious.

Sometimes God sends us to places for us to cause a positive shift. You cannot shift a hurtful and religious place while staying at home. Again, I am not saying to attend places of abuse and places that are really dens of thieves. All I am saying is that if we are truly going to be like Jesus, we must not allow the diabolical acts of others to be our excuses not to gather anywhere faithfully. If you cannot gather "here," make sure you gather "there." No excuses!

Secondly and primarily, as it relates to a kingdom, all kingdoms have a military. If you claim to be a part of God's military—if you claim to be an apostle, or any role identified with the Kingdom of God, and you are not under any human spiritual authority, then you are operating illegally. If we do the work of the military (preach, cast out devils, engage in spiritual warfare, etc.), we should report back to base—to our commander or our persons of accountability.

That is Kingdom. Kingdom is orderly. Kingdom means accountability. Kingdom is apostolic; it is a sending form of government. In fact, it is a GOVERNment. Therefore, if you are not being governed by God's human representatives, you are not aligning with the Government of the King. Remember, the King has human authorities that govern His military on earth, such as generals, colonels, lieutenants, majors, captains, and so forth. No matter how anointed you are and what your calling is in the Kingdom of God, if you are not accountable to authority, you are not in the King's will. Even a general is under authority. Soldiers have different bases as to where they are 1) trained, 2) sent, and 3) assigned to report back to. This is the Economy of God.

The Twelve Apostles of the Lamb were all accountable to each other. They did not do whatever they wanted to do. As a matter of fact, when Paul was converted, Jesus told Ananias that Saul was a chosen vessel to bear His name before the Gentiles. That was in Acts chapter nine. But it was not until Acts chapter thirteen, approximately fourteen to seventeen years later, when the leaders of the Church laid hands on him and commissioned him, that he was launched into his apostolic ministry. See, although Jesus commissioned him in chapter nine, he had to be released by human authority in chapter thirteen. That is indeed the Kingdom of God protocol. We will discuss this further as we continue through this book.

Friends, this is not to condemn anyone. However, if we are going to be a Kingdom, we must be a Kingdom. Let us repent and do what the King has required of His citizens. Some things are the law of religion. However, other things are the Law of the Kingdom. Let us not conflate the two.

MYTH #3

An Apostle Is the Highest Rank in the Kingdom of God.

And God hath set some in the church, first apostles, secondarily prophets, thirdly teachers, after that miracles, then gifts of healings, helps, governments, diversities of tongues.
—1 Corinthians 12:28

There is neither Jew nor Greek, there is neither bond nor free, there is neither male nor female: for ye are all one in Christ Jesus.
—Galatians 3:28

---

1 Corinthians 12:28 says that God has placed apostles first in the Church. *Prōton* is the Greek word that is used here for the word *first*. This word does not mean first in the power structure but first in sequence. Apostles were first in sequence as it relates to the order of the formation of the Church. However, as it relates to ecclesiastical order and governance, the apostle of a specific church or of a specific fellowship is the senior leader of that specific church. If the apostle of a particular local church has appointed a pastor to lead that particular congregation, if that pastor is going to be successful, the apostle should empower him or her to be the senior leadership face of that ministry. For clarity, this is in the instance that the apostle is the establishmentarian of a given church.

However, although the senior pastor becomes *the set man* of that church, that apostle is still the father of that church and of that pastor. In other words, the apostle (if establishmentarian) serves as the CEO, *Chief Executive Officer*, while the pastor serves as the COO, *Chief Operating Officer*.

In the governing of the Church, the apostle "may" have greater responsibility in a specific church if he is an establishmentarian. He may have greater responsibility in a fellowship if he is an establishmentarian or presiding prelate. Whoever has greater responsibility has greater preeminence in the jurisdiction that he or she is assigned to. Let us take it further. You can be an apostle who lives in Orlando, but not be an apostle or "the" apostle of Orlando. Your assignment and responsibilities can lie elsewhere.

Furthermore, just because you are an apostle does not mean that you outrank everyone else. If you attend a local church, for which you are not responsible, the pastor of that congregation outranks you in that territory, for they are the senior leader in that sector. Whoever has greater responsibility in a particular domain has greater authority in that domain.

In the Church, one can have greater authority and preeminence than another. However, in the Kingdom of God, we are all equal. This can be confusing because many of us do not know the difference between the Church of God and the Kingdom of God. Some of us think the two are synonymous, while others think that the two roles are distinct. This will be discussed further.

There are individuals who say things like, "Come out of the Church and step into the Kingdom." Or, "There is a difference between Church folk and Kingdom folk." This is anti-Scripture and borderline anti-Christ. If what you mean is that there is a difference between religious folk and Kingdom folk, then say that. Also, if that is truly what you mean, then you can also say that there is a difference between religious folk and Church folk. Oftentimes, we do more harm than good using such proclamations with erroneous definitions.

What Is the Ekklesia?

You may well ask: is the Church an institution with a head and a religious hierarchy? The conversation below between Jesus and Peter is enlightening.

And Simon Peter answered and said, Thou art the Christ, the Son of the living God. And Jesus answered and said unto him, Blessed art thou, Simon Barjona: for flesh and blood hath not revealed it unto thee, but my Father which is in heaven. And I say also unto thee, That thou art Peter, and upon this rock I will build my church; and the gates of hell shall not prevail against it.
—Matthew 16:16-18

More often, individuals damn and dog the Church because their demon-inspired definition of the Church is a man-made building where religious practices occur. When you have this as your definition of the Church, your perspective of the Church will always be faulty. Christ's Church is not a facility. The Greek word for *church* is *ekklesia*, and it means *the called-out ones*. Who are the called-out ones? You and I as followers of Christ. The Church is not an institution, but it is an organism of united believers.

The Bride of Christ

The Church is also the Bride of Christ.

And there came unto me one of the seven angels which had the seven vials full of the seven last plagues, and talked with me, saying, Come hither, I will shew thee the bride, the Lamb's wife.
—Revelation 21:9

Think about this: if you are so close to Jesus, and His Word tells you in many different instances that the Church is His Bride, do you think He is okay with you harassing her? What real husband would be close to someone who insults his bride? Speaking personally, my bride is the most precious human being on this earth to me. If someone is trying to be close to me but is speaking negatively about my wife, we are going to have a real problem. Whenever you are anti-Church, you are also anti-Christ, and many of us need to repent. You cannot bless the Groom and threaten His Bride.

So when we say things like, "Leave the Church and come on into the Kingdom," what kingdom are you talking about? If you are telling people to stop being a part of Christ's Bride, the only kingdom they have a choice to go to is the kingdom of hell. You cannot be a part of the Kingdom of God if you are not a part of the Church, Christ's Bride.

Now, if you want people to leave the spirit of religion, just say that. Whenever you are not accurate with your statements, you can actually lead others astray.

The Legislative Governing Body

Also, notice that Jesus states: "[. . .] *and upon this rock I will build my church; and the gates of hell shall not prevail against it.*" As mentioned, the word *church* here in the Greek is the word *ekklesia*, referring to those who are called out. It was never a religious term in the day that Jesus used it. This term was a common governmental term.

In ancient Greece, the *ekklesia*[12] was a "called-out" assembly of citizens in a city-state who had final control over policy, the right to hear appeals in the public court, take part in the election of chief magistrates, and confer special privileges on individuals. In other words, the *ekklesia* was the legislative governing body of a particular city-state in ancient Greece.

This is why when Jesus told Peter that upon this rock He would build His *ekklesia*, Peter knew exactly what that term meant. Understanding the history of this word will grant you a better understanding of what the Church really is. The Church is the legislative governing body of the Kingdom of God.

"I thought the church was a hospital!" some would say. God never said that. The place that some have incorrectly called "church" might serve as a hospital in times of need, but the Church, Christ's Bride, is the governing Body of the Kingdom.

What Are the Characteristics of the Kingdom of God?

For a kingdom to exist and function as a kingdom, it must possess eight characteristics. The Kingdom of God also possesses these characteristics, as given by the late great Dr. Myles Munroe[13]. Please see his insights below, which are integrated with words of my own.

1. **A King**

    A *King*-dom is the King's domain. The Kingdom of God, therefore, possesses a king, and that King is Christ. Being a king is unlike being a president. A king cannot be voted out of power. A king has the final authority. Whatever a king says is law.

2. **A Territory**

    Every kingdom must have a territory. The essence of a kingdom is property or land. The word *kingdom*, in fact, is a fusion of two words—king and domain, a domain or territory over which a king rules. Christ is Lord *over* all, but not Lord *of* all.

3. **Constitution**

The third characteristic of a kingdom is a constitution. A constitution is a body of laws that guides the governance of the kingdom. Many people believe America is a democracy. However, America is not purely a democracy. America is a democratic republic. Do you remember the Pledge of Allegiance? "And to the republic for which it stands . . ." America is a democratic republic.

Unlike the constitution of a republic or a democracy, a kingdom's constitution is the document that constitutes the king's desire for his citizens. It contains the responsibilities, laws, rights, and privileges of the people. It cannot be changed by the people, and the king himself is subject to the dictates of the constitution. The Bible is the constitution of the Kingdom of God.

4. **Laws**

The constitution contains the laws of the kingdom. Kingdom laws are not rules and regulations. They are not difficult codes aimed at subjecting everyone. Its laws are statements of boundaries within which we are free to thrive, prosper, and reach our full potential. These laws carry within themselves consequences. This means that when you break a law, God does not punish you, but the law punishes you. Whatever God (the king) says is law.

5. **Citizens**

Every kingdom must possess citizens. The king decides who is a citizen of the kingdom and how anyone can become a citizen. We enter the Kingdom of Heaven through the process that Jesus called being *born again*—changing our mind and turning from our rebellion against God, placing our trust in Jesus for the forgiveness of our rebellion, and acknowledging Him as Lord (King) of our lives. This *new birth* makes us *the Church*, whereby we become citizens of the Kingdom of God. I hope you are beginning to understand our privileged position. The citizenship we receive through the new birth is citizenship by naturalization because we are *born again*, born into the Kingdom of God.

6. **Rights and Privileges**

   Every citizen in the kingdom is entitled to rights and privileges. As citizens of the Kingdom of God, our rights and privileges are contained in the Bible (the constitution). They are the promises God has made to us concerning us. Remember, whatever God says is law, and the king abides by the laws he creates. So, God abides by His laws and, of necessity, has to fulfill His promises to you according to the law. If you are not seeing any of the rights and privileges manifesting in your life, you should place a petition in the courtroom of the Kingdom of God through prayer.

7. **Army**

   Every kingdom must also possess an army. These are the forces that protect and defend the citizens of the kingdom. It is great that we are citizens of God's Kingdom, the ones to be protected and not the army. The angels are the army of God's Kingdom. They are charged with the responsibility of guarding the citizens, the Church.

8. **Commonwealth**

   Next, every kingdom has a commonwealth. A righteous and benevolent king does not amass wealth for himself but uses it for the welfare of his citizens. This is why it is only in a kingdom that we truly find common wealth; that is, the wealth is common to all the people. In the Kingdom of God, **every citizen has equal access** to the resources of God's Kingdom. There are no special or preferred citizens. There is no hierarchy in the Kingdom!

Those are the characteristics of a kingdom, but we still have not defined what the Kingdom of God is. My pastor states that the Kingdom of God is "Reality as God prescribed it." In the reality that God prescribed, there is no inferiority/superiority among people. We work in collaboration with one another.

So when Paul says, "*There is neither Jew nor Greek, there is neither bond nor free, there is neither male nor female: for ye are all one in Christ Jesus,*" he could have also soundly said, "*There is neither clergy nor laity, there is neither apostle nor pastor . . .*"

Therefore, just because you are an apostle does not mean that you are ranked higher than someone else. You are no closer to God being an apostle than you are being an usher. I quote my pastor, Bishop Michael Blue, again when he says, "The highest rank in the Kingdom of God is 'son of God.'" We are not talking about gender. Being a son of God is a status. The Gospel of John 1:12 says, "But as many as received him, to them gave he power to become the sons of God, even to them that believe on his name." If you are in God, you are deemed a son of God. Ladies, do not be alarmed. If males have to be the Bride of Christ, females can equally be sons of God. There is no higher rank in the Kingdom of God than son of God. Praise God!

MYTH #4

Having the Title Means That One Is.

Having the title does not mean one is an apostle. This is obvious. To further elaborate, people may even call you an *apostle*, although you are not one. If that is what you call yourself, many will echo it out of respect for you. But remember, just because people affirm you, it does not mean they affirm what you call yourself.

By the same token, just because someone does not wear the title *apostle*, it does not mean that he or she is not one. Imagine what more we would have received and accomplished if we had acknowledged that great servants of God, such as Martin Luther (of the Protestant Reformation) and John Wesley (of the First Great Awakening), were indeed apostles. You will see why they were indeed apostles as you continue to read this book prayerfully. A tree is known by the fruit it bears, not by the title it wears.

MYTH #5

A False Apostle Is Always a False Christian.

A false apostle is not necessarily a false Christian. If one is a false apostle by deception, then, yes, he or she is also a false Christian. If one is a false apostle by being misinformed as to what an apostle is, then they are not necessarily a false Christian. You can be a true Christian and misguidedly attempt to enter the wrong office.

MYTH #6

You Have To Be a Certain Age To Be an Apostle.

Understandably, we may become concerned with those who are young in age who carry certain lofty titles. Many times, such appointments are not even practical, feasible, or appropriate. However, just as the young must be careful with these titles, others must be careful not to allow what we call *practical* to come against what is indeed *biblical.*

If we study some prominent substantive scholars, they suggest the Twelve Apostles of the Lamb were probably all in their late teens or early twenties, with the possible exception of the apostle Peter. However, before they were apostles and were solely disciples, it is believed that they were in their mid to late teens. There is much scriptural and historical evidence for this claim, and we will give you just a few basic examples.

In Luke 3:23, we learn that Jesus was about thirty years old when He started public ministry. In the Jewish culture, disciples were younger than their teacher. As a consequence, we can reason that the disciples of Christ were younger than He. Also, remember that Jesus often called them *"little children,"* possibly because they were much younger than He was—at least the majority of them.

Also, in Matthew 17:24-27, Jesus and His disciples went to Capernaum, and the collectors of the two-drachma temple tax came to Peter and asked, "Doesn't your teacher pay the temple tax?" Jesus instructed Peter to go fishing. When Peter caught a fish, the fish had a four-drachma coin in its mouth, enough to pay the taxes for Jesus and Peter. Please note that the tax only had to be paid by those who were at least twenty years of age. Why were the other disciples' taxes not paid for? Perhaps it was because they were still teenagers. There are many more scriptural and historical reasons to believe that the twelve apostles were in their teens. I would encourage you to do further study of it[14].

The point is that, if the majority of the original twelve were likely in their teens as disciples and in their twenties as apostles, we must not dispute the fact that God can presently use younger individuals to be apostles, bishops, and other officeholders. Maturity is necessary for apostolic ministry, and some maturity is or should be correlated to years. Serving in a Kingdom of God office is not about AGE, but rather about STAGE (maturity).

MYTH #7

Seeing Jesus Makes One an Apostle.

Wherefore of these men which have companied with us all the time that the Lord Jesus went in and out among us, Beginning from the baptism of John, unto that same day that he was taken up from us, must one be ordained to be a witness with us of his resurrection. And they appointed two, Joseph called Barsabas, who was surnamed Justus, and Matthias. And they prayed, and said, Thou, Lord, which knowest the hearts of all men, shew whether of these two thou hast chosen, That he may take part of this ministry and apostleship, from which Judas by transgression fell, that he might go to his own place. And they gave forth their lots; and the lot fell upon Matthias; and he was numbered with the eleven apostles.

—Acts 1:21-26

This myth might be the most challenging for some. However, I stand by it. Seeing Christ through a dream, a vision, or even through an apparition of Him does not necessarily define one as an apostle.

Scripturally, during Jesus's ministry, He had seventy disciples. Out of the seventy, only twelve were His apostles. You could possibly even say thirteen because Matthias took the place of Judas. The point is, these seventy saw Jesus and were taught by Jesus, but the majority of them were not deemed one of the Twelve Apostles of the Lamb.

Even in the first chapter of Acts, the Apostles had a conviction to appoint someone to the apostolic seat that Judas forfeited. The requirement was that this individual had to have been with them and Jesus the entire time since His baptism and resurrection. There were two candidates, Joseph and Matthias, and Matthias was chosen because there was a vacancy for only one. Joseph evidently saw Jesus, but was not chosen as an apostle.

So, it is not solely seeing Jesus that makes one an apostle. The question is: if or when you saw Jesus, what was the mission that He gave you? If your encounter with Jesus did not come with an apostolic commissioning, He was not calling you as an apostle. Jesus being a *Seen One* does not make you an apostle. Jesus commissioning you as a *sent one* does.

Please understand the conviction of true apostles. Apostles are moved by mission. There is a mission from the Lord that consumes them, not so much a vision of the Lord.

MYTH #8

"Prophecy" Makes You an Apostle.

Friends, someone *prophesying* to you that you are an apostle does not make you one. It takes more than a prophecy for you to be an apostle. Some people prophesy assumptions; others falsely prophesy our own desires. We must be very careful trying to forcibly walk into something that someone declares over our lives.

Let me share this as well. In my early to mid-twenties, people would prophesy to me that I was an apostle. They possibly heard right, but *I* must hear right. I had apostolic gifting, but I did not have apostolic maturity. I was not mature enough to walk in the office of apostle.

Oftentimes, people will prophesy the grace that they see on you when, in fact, they do not see the character that is in you. You can have apostolic, prophetic, evangelistic, pastoral, and didactic grace, but if you are not mature in the character and charisma of that grace, you are not ready to walk in that specific office. Fivefold grace is for all believers. Fivefold office is only for the mature. This is why it took Paul fourteen to seventeen years to be commissioned as an apostle, because he had a lot of learning and growing to do.

We will elaborate on this further in the next chapter.

CHAPTER

04

WHAT IS AN APOSTLE?

The word *apostle* comes from the Greek word *apóstolos*. This word is a compound of the preposition *apo* (meaning *from, away from,* or *off*) and the verb *stello* (meaning *send*). *Apóstolos* literally means *one who is sent away*. However, if you simply look at the definition of the word, you will never know the fullness of its meaning. We are all sent by God to do His work. However, we are not all apostles. As you see, the general definition itself is not enough to understand the actual meaning.

Like the term *church* or *ekklesia*, the term *apostle* was not a religious term when Jesus used it in His day. As a matter of fact, this term even predates the New Testament. The word *apóstolos* was a governmental term used by the Greeks in different ways.

I. **The Admiral of a Fleet**

Between the years 384 and 322 BC, the Greeks used this word to relate to an admiral of a fleet of ships who was sent out by his emperor to establish his rulership and government in foreign territories[15]. To be totally accurate, *apóstolos* was not only used to describe the admiral, but also the fleet of ships and the crew who accompanied him. It was the apostle and his crew's job to replicate their civilization, government, and culture in other areas and regions all over the world. They were not to colonize areas that were already colonized with Greek communities and culture. Rather, it was the apostles' assignment to go where the barbarians were. Their assignment was to conquer the territory of the uncivilized.

This was a very daunting and dangerous task. The only reason someone would dare desire to be an apostle was simply because they represented the emperor. To be in a strange land among the heathen was life-threatening. This admiral, this apostle, and his *apostolic* team had to teach the natives their language, their culture, their customs, and laws. The apostle also had to direct the building of infrastructure, including houses and roads. Once this difficult task was completed, the apostle and his apostolic team would get on the ship, travel to another region, and do it again.

That is why when Jesus called His disciples His *apóstolos*, they knew exactly what it meant. He used a governmental term so they would immediately understand their function and assignment. Apostles are sent by the King to go into territories occupied by sinners to establish the King's government, civilization, and culture. Once the foundation has been solidified, the apostle and his team leave that territory to go and establish the King's Kingdom somewhere else.

2. **A Passport**

    Over time, since the term *apóstolos* was so closely identified with traveling to distant lands, it also became synonymous with *passport*[16]. If an individual desired to enter or exit a country, he was required to present a legal document called *apóstolos*. With this document, one had the right and the ability to travel from place to place.

Even now, the US Department of State uses a term called *apostille* that is closely associated with foreign travel. An *apostille* certifies a document so that foreign countries will recognize it. Do you see the similarity?

Some have said that when Jesus used the term *apóstolos*, it implied that an apostle would be a spiritual passport that enables believers' rite of passage to deeper spiritual truths. This may very well be true. My spiritual life has grown the most by serving under an authentic apostle. However, if not careful, this view can help to esteem the apostle more than is warranted. Remember, this high view of the apostle as one of honor should not be allowed to escalate to superiority or idolatry.

I like to say that when Jesus used this term, He also had in mind that an apostle would be a spiritual passport and rite of passage not for people, but for Christ. The apostle is Christ's passport and rite of passage to territories in which Christ is not known or not known well. Some might say, "This is what evangelists do." Not necessarily. The work of the apostle and the evangelist intersect and are akin in some respects, but they are not synonymous. Evangelists win lost people. Apostles win lost territory. Apostles are the passport for

Christ to come into a system, a territory, and a region for "Kingdom of God" formation or reformation.

This is why certain Christian leaders can be in a particular community, state, or region for years and find that certain avenues they have tried to get access to never seem to be possible. However, when an apostle arrives, what others had been attempting in vain to do, this person is the one who gets access. It is not because one is more anointed than the other. It is simply because an apostle has a different grace or anointing. In territories where other people may struggle, apostles excel. When you do not have a passport, many borders and territories are closed to you. Certain borders only open up to apostles because apostles are passports. Think of it this way—a passport is essentially a key to a foreign door. The apostolic grace is indeed a door-opening grace.

3. **A Fully Empowered Ambassador**

    The Greek historian Herodotus and the Greek philosopher Aristotle both used the term *apóstolos* to describe the sending off of powerful individuals, such as an *ambassador*. An ambassador was a high-ranking diplomat who was sent out on a specific mission in a foreign land to represent a government or king[17]. When Jesus called His Twelve Disciples apostles, it was not with the idea of clergymen but rather ambassadors.

Ambassadors came with the same authority as the one who sent them. The sender gave the ambassador full power to represent them in a foreign land. Therefore, to attack the king's *apóstolos* is to wage war against the king's entire government.

A Working Definition

These three ways in which the term *apóstolos* was commonly used hundreds of years before Jesus ever did give us a better understanding of what an apostle truly is.

I therefore extract a working definition of an apostle as follows:

> *An apostle is a fully empowered and authorized ambassador sent by and on behalf of Christ to go into foreign territories where Christ is not known, or known well, to establish or reestablish Kingdom of God government, civilization, and culture. Once the foundation has been solidified, the apostle and his or her apostolic team leave that territory to go and establish or reestablish Christ's government, civilization, and culture somewhere else.*

That, my friends, is a working definition of what an apostle is. For the many who claim apostleship, the question is, does their life look like this definition?

I urge you to watch Paramount Pictures' *Gladiator II* for the sake of understanding, to a small degree, what an apostle was in ancient Greece. This is not an endorsement. However, it is a relatively clean movie, and I have a personal affinity toward ancient Greek and Greek mythological films.

In the second scene, General Acacius sets sail, accompanied by hundreds of Roman ships, to lead an army of Roman troops to conquer a city in ancient Africa Nova on behalf of the Roman Empire.

Acacius, leading Rome, breaks through the city's wall. After hours of battle and bloodshed, Acacius, on behalf of Rome, conquers the city. After a victorious battle, he declares, "I claim this city for the glory of Rome." The character Acacius actually depicts an ancient *apostle* of Rome. By the way, the Kingdom of God does not exert physical force or any other kind of coercion. Therefore, I want it to be clear that I am not endorsing violence. I am simply explaining what an apostle was in that culture.

Apostles of Christ penetrate the walls of an assigned territory and invest years of blood, sweat, and tears in battle to conquer that territory and then declare, "I claim this territory for the glory of God."

05

FOURTEEN MARKS OF AN APOSTLE

We now have a better historical and scriptural lens to know what an apostle is. Although the definition and the historical understanding of what an apostle originally was help us with identifying true apostles, we still need to discuss some of the signs, or marks, of an apostle.

These signs and marks amount to fourteen.

I. **Real apostles are willing to forfeit their freedoms and rights to prevent being a stumbling block so the gospel can be received by others.**

Am I am not an apostle? Am I not free? Have I not seen Jesus Christ our Lord? Are not ye my work in the Lord? If I be not an apostle unto others, yet doubtless I am to you: for the seal of mine apostleship are ye in the Lord. Mine answer to them that do examine me is this, Have we not power to eat and to drink? Have we not power to lead about a sister, a wife, as well as other apostles, and as the brethren of the Lord, and Cephas? Or I only and Barnabas, have not we power to forbear working? Who goeth a warfare any time at his own charges? Who planteth a vineyard, and eateth not of the fruit thereof? Or who feedeth a flock, and eateth not of the milk of the flock? Say I these things as a man? Or saith not the law the same also? For it is written in the law of Moses, thou shalt not muzzle the mouth of the ox that treadeth out the corn. Doth God take care for oxen? Or saith he it altogether for our sakes? For our sakes, no doubt, this is written: that he that ploweth should plow in hope; and that he that thresheth in hope should be partaker of his hope. If we have sown unto you spiritual things, is it a great thing if we shall reap your carnal things? If others be partakers of this power over you, are not we rather?
Nevertheless we have not used this power; but suffer all things, lest we should hinder the gospel of Christ. Do ye not know that they which minister about holy things live of the things of the temple? and they which wait at the altar are partakers with the altar? Even so hath the Lord ordained that they which preach the gospel should live of the gospel. But I have used none of these things: neither have I written

these things, that it should be so done unto me: for it were better for me to die, than that any man should make my glorying void. For though I preach the gospel, I have nothing to glory of: for necessity is laid upon me; yea, woe is unto me, if I preach not the gospel! For if I do this thing willingly, I have a reward: but if against my will, a dispensation of the gospel is committed unto me. What is my reward then? Verily that, when I preach the gospel, I may make the gospel of Christ without charge, that I abuse not my power in the gospel. For though I be free from all men, yet have I made myself servant unto all, that I might gain the more. And unto the Jews I became as a Jew, that I might gain the Jews; to them that are under the law, as under the law, that I might gain them that are under the law; To them that are without law, as without law, (being not without law to God, but under the law to Christ,) that I might gain them that are without law. To the weak became I as weak, that I might gain the weak: I am made all things to all men, that I might by all means save some.

—**1 Corinthians 9:1-22**

Many believe that the apostle Paul is defending his apostleship in this passage. As you see, in the King James Version, the chapter begins with, *"Am I not an apostle?"* However, Paul is not merely defending his apostleship in this chapter. In the original handwritten copies of the Scripture, the first question is not *"Am I not an apostle?"* but rather *"Am I not free?"*

The entire chapter is in defense of his first question, *"Am I not free?"* Having this understanding of what the scriptures read originally helps our understanding of Paul's defense. Let us read it again in the New English Translation.

Am I not free? Am I not an apostle? Have I not seen Jesus our Lord? Are you not my work in the Lord? If I am not an apostle to others, at least I am to you, for you are the confirming sign of my apostleship in the Lord. This is my defense to those who examine me. Do we not have the right to financial support? Do we not have the right to the company of a believing wife, like the other apostles and the Lord's brothers and Cephas? Or do only Barnabas and I lack the right not to work?

Who ever serves in the army at his own expense? Who plants a vineyard and does not eat its fruit? Who tends a flock and does not consume its milk? Am I saying these things only on the basis of common sense, or does the law not say this as well? For it is written in the law of Moses, **"Do not muzzle an ox while it is treading out the grain."** God is not concerned here about oxen, is he? Or is he not surely speaking for our benefit? It was written for us, because the one plowing and threshing ought to work in hope of enjoying the harvest.

If we sowed spiritual blessings among you, is it too much to reap material things from you? If others receive this right from you, are we not more deserving?

But we have not made use of this right. Instead we endure everything so that we may not be a hindrance to the gospel of Christ. Don't you know that those who serve in the temple eat food from the temple, and those who serve at the altar receive a part of the offerings? In the same way the Lord commanded those who proclaim the gospel to receive their living by the gospel. But I have not used any of these rights. And I am not writing these things so that something will be done for me. In fact, it would be better for me to die than—no one will deprive me of my reason for boasting!

For if I preach the gospel, I have no reason for boasting, because I am compelled to do this. Woe to me if I do not preach the gospel! For if I do this voluntarily, I have a reward. But if I do it unwillingly, I am entrusted with a responsibility. What then is my reward? That when I preach the gospel I may offer the gospel free of charge, and so not make full use of my rights in the gospel.

For since I am free from all I can make myself a slave to all, in order to gain even more people. To the Jews I became like a Jew to gain the Jews. To those under the law I became like one under the law (though I myself am not under the law) to gain those under the law. To those free from the law I became like one free from the law (though I am not free from God's law but under the law of Christ) to gain those free from the law. To the weak I became weak in order to gain the weak. I have become all things to all people, so that by all means I may save some.

— 1 **Corinthians 9:1-22 NET**

Again, Paul is not so much defending his apostleship as he is defending his freedom as an apostle. The question, *"Am I not free?"* has to do with the liberties he has as a Christian, but particularly as an apostle. He has the same rights that all other apostles have but yet he chooses to be voided of them. Do you see?

When he asks, *"Am I not an apostle?"* it is in defense, not of his apostleship, but of his rights and liberties. In other words, if I am an apostle like them, if I have seen Christ like them, if I have established a church full of new converts like them, then why am I robbed of the same liberties that they enjoy? If I have the right to be blessed financially by the Church like they are blessed financially by the Church, why then am I not blessed financially through the Church? If I have the right to have a wife like the other apostles have a wife, why then do I not enjoy my rights?

Paul goes on to share that he has not demanded his rights because he would rather suffer without the things he is deserving of if it is going to be a hindrance to people receiving the Gospel. Although he is free (*at liberty*), he has made himself a slave so that he can save the lives of others for the cause of Christ.

That, my friends, is a sign of an apostle. Apostles, especially the more mature apostles, will forfeit what they deserve because of small-minded people. They would rather struggle without the blessings due to them than be a stumbling block to others. They would rather earn their own income outside of the church than allow the church to go under financially. They would rather drive a regular car than a luxury car just so they can come against any spirit that might accuse them of church thievery or materialism. Real apostles will die so that others may live.

Too many of those who seek apostleship do not realize that the call is not an elevation of status, but a demotion of death. Think of the apostolic grace as actually a grace to be disgraced. You have the grace to be despised, humiliated, and mistreated.

I hate this for Paul, but I do not hate his sacrifice. I hate the fact that because he is so meek, humble, and sacrificial regarding the church at Corinth, the church dishonors him. Because he is the one they are familiar with, they honor the other apostles more than they honor the one who established them. Friends, the relationships that are most fruitful are relationships of mutual honor.

True *mature* apostles do not want to be a burden to those they lead (serve). They would much rather bear the burdens of those whom they lead. They will forfeit their own rights so they will not be an impediment to the Gospel. How beautiful—how honorable!

Let us look at another passage.

Have I committed an offence in abasing myself that ye might be exalted, because I have preached to you the gospel of God freely? I robbed other churches, taking wages of them, to do you service. And when I was present with you, and wanted, I was chargeable to no man: for that which was lacking to me the brethren which came from Macedonia supplied: and in all things I have kept myself from being burdensome unto you, and so will I keep myself.
But what I do, that I will do, that I may cut off occasion from them which desire occasion; that wherein they glory, they may be found even as we. For such are false apostles, deceitful workers, transforming themselves into the apostles of Christ.
—2 Corinthians 11:7-9;12-13

Paul says that he humbled himself so that the church could be exalted. That is the maturity and humility of an apostle. He is sacrificing his own privileges so that the church will be blessed. Some preachers might say, "I am not going to do all that." Or, "They are gonna pay me my honorarium." The preacher who says those types of things is not an apostle!

As a matter of fact, the apostle Paul says that he will continue to be sacrificial in this way. That will prove that those who glory in calling themselves apostles but do not sacrifice as he does are actually false apostles. Please listen! If those who claim to be apostles are not giving up their liberties for the betterment of people, then it is proof that they are false apostles. That is what Paul said. That is the Bible.

Let us look at one more.

Behold, the third time I am ready to come to you; and I will not be burdensome to you: for I seek not yours, but you: for the children ought not to lay up for the parents, but the parents for the children.
—2 Corinthians 12:14

This is indeed an apostolic verse. Do you see the passion of an apostle? Do you see the heart of an apostolic father? Paul is not coming for an honorarium. Would he accept one? Of course. However, he does not want to put a financial burden on the church. Apostles do not look to be taken care of. They look to take care of the Church. Apostles are true parents of sacrifice.

Moreover, Paul accepted gifts from other churches but not the Corinthian Church, because the Corinthian Church could have made it seem that Paul only served them for profit. Paul denies his freedom for the sake of the Gospel. He is not motivated by financial gain.

A true apostle will honor a church by not being a financial burden, and an honorable apostolic church will not leave its apostle financially burdened as well. It is all about mutual honor.

Here is another sign.

2. **Patience**

---

*Truly the signs of an apostle were wrought among you in all **patience**, in signs, and wonders, and mighty deeds.*
—2 Corinthians 12:12

Paul shares with the church at Corinth that they have witnessed him work the signs of an apostle. The first sign that he indicates is patience. The word patience here is the Greek word *hypomone*. This word means *steadfastness, consistency,* and *endurance.* It speaks to one's ability to remain in position.

True apostolic work is difficult. Establishing a Kingdom of God civilization in heathen territory can be exhausting and at times discouraging. And Satan throws everything your way when you are truly doing apostolic work. He does not want to lose territory that he occupies. He wants the apostles to quit! He will bring about discouragement from within their church, slander, spiritual attacks on their family, financial hardships, attacks from envious clergy, and temptations to serve at already well-established churches.

A sign that you are truly an apostle is staying power. That is what patience means in this text, "Staying on the frontlines in spite of . . ." Apostles do not stay in a particular territory forever. However, they do stay until the foundation has been laid or reformed.

Any individual who claims to be an apostle but does not possess stickability is not one. If they are not consistent, if they keep canceling worship services, they are not an apostle. If they are always opening a church and then closing it, they are not an apostle. Apostles continue to plow in spite of the obstacles. Apostles persevere in the midst of persecution. Consider 2 Corinthians 11:23-30:

Are they ministers of Christ? (I speak as a fool) I am more; in labours more abundant, in stripes above measure, in prisons more frequent, in deaths oft. Of the Jews five times received I forty stripes save one. Thrice was I beaten with rods, once was I stoned, thrice I suffered shipwreck, a night and a day I have been in the deep; In journeyings often, in perils of waters, in perils of robbers, in perils by mine own countrymen, in perils by the heathen, in perils in the city, in perils in the wilderness, in perils in the sea, in perils among false brethren; In weariness and painfulness, in watchings often, in hunger and thirst, in fastings often, in cold and nakedness.
Beside those things that are without, that which cometh upon me daily, the care of all the churches. Who is weak, and I am not weak? who is offended, and I burn not? If I must needs glory, I will glory of the things which concern mine infirmities.
—2 Corinthians 11:23-30

Despite all that the apostle Paul went through, he remained patient. Apostles will continue doing the work.

3. Signs

---

*Truly the signs of an apostle were wrought among you in all patience, in **signs**, and wonders, and mighty deeds.*
—2 Corinthians 12:12

Signs are then the mark of an apostle. A sign (Greek *semeion*) is a supernatural witness that authenticates that one is sent by God. If souls are not being saved, bodies are not being healed, devils are not being cast out, and any measure of godly supernatural sign is absent, one is not an apostle.

4. Wonders

---

*Truly the signs of an apostle were wrought among you in all patience, in signs, and **wonders**, and mighty deeds.*
—2 Corinthians 12:12

All wonders are signs, but not all signs are necessarily wonders. *Wonders* in the Greek text is *téras*. The Latin source is *miraculum*, which means *object of wonder*. A wonder or miracle is a supernatural sign that defies nature. It goes against the natural law and leaves the witnesses in wonder. Miracles are wonders. Prophecy is a sign, but it is not a miracle or wonder. Speaking in tongues is a sign, but it is not a wonder. Yes, speaking in tongues is intriguing, fascinating even, but it is not categorically a miracle. Casting out devils is a sign, but it is not a wonder. If it is not categorically a miracle, then it is not a wonder.

A wonder is something so extraordinary that it causes bewilderment. It causes people to marvel. Wonders are a shock factor among their witnesses. They provoke the fear of God.

The New Testament reminds us that Christ and His Apostles (through the power of the Holy Spirit) appropriated not merely *signs* of God's power, but a combination of *signs and wonders*.

Let us look at just a few places in only the Book of Acts where we see miracles or wonders:

- Acts 5:15: People are being healed just by contact with Peter's shadow.

- Acts 5:17-25; 12:5-11; 16:25-30: There are three miraculous prison breaks.

- Acts 8:39: The Holy Spirit miraculously snatches Philip and transports him to another location after he witnesses to and baptizes an Ethiopian eunuch.

- Acts 14:8-10: A man who had been a cripple since birth is healed under the ministry of Paul.

- Acts 19:11-12: People are delivered from devils and are healed through the administration of handkerchiefs and aprons that have been placed or rubbed on their bodies.

- Acts 20:9-12: A man falls asleep and falls out of a third-story window to his death while Paul is preaching. God uses Paul to bring him back to life.

These are just a few examples of wonders found in the Book of Acts alone. I can recall a wonder that happened not too long ago at one of our church locations. At the beginning of the service, one of the church members told us that they had just found their nephew (less than two years old) in a pond. The medical professionals said that he had been there for at least twenty minutes. When they brought him out of the pond, he was dead.

We began to pray for him during the service. About ten minutes later, the church member received a call during the service that the precious child was alive and well. That is a wonder. Praise be to God!

If there is no history of wonders that have occurred in an individual's ministry, whether in large measure or small, according to Scripture, he or she is not an apostle.

---

*Truly the signs of an apostle were wrought among you in all patience, in signs, and wonders, and **mighty deeds**.*
—2 Corinthians 12:12

As you can see, I did not include mighty deeds (Greek *dunamis*) as another sign of an apostle. Mighty deeds are not an additional sign. Mighty deeds are an amplifying term for wonders. The word *and* in this text is the Greek word *kai*. Depending on the context, this word can be translated as *and, also, even, both, then, so,* or *likewise*. I am of the strong opinion that, as it relates to mighty deeds, the word *kai* here should be translated as *even*. In other words, Paul was saying that these wonders were *in fact* mighty deeds. Mighty deeds are not distinct from wonders but are rather an elaboration that they are indeed wonders.

5.   **A Unique Vision/Revelation of Christ**

And Simon Peter answered and said, Thou art the Christ, the Son of the living God. And Jesus answered and said unto him, Blessed art thou, Simon Barjona: for flesh and blood hath not revealed it unto thee, but my Father which is in heaven. And I say also unto thee, That thou art Peter, and upon this rock I will build my church; and the gates of hell shall not prevail against it.
Matthew 16:16-18

Am I not an apostle? am I not free? have I not seen Jesus Christ our Lord? are not ye my work in the Lord?
—1 Corinthians 9:1

And did all drink the same spiritual drink: for they drank of that spiritual Rock that followed them: and that Rock was Christ.
—1 Corinthians 10:4

But I certify you, brethren, that the gospel which was preached of me is not after man. For I neither received it of man, neither was I taught it, but by the revelation of Jesus Christ.
—Galatians 1:11-12

True apostles have had a unique vision or revelation of Jesus Christ. They may also have had a unique encounter or encounters with Christ. Although it is not the exclusive factor of apostleship, it is an element of the ministry of the apostle. The persistent question is, "Does one have to have literally seen Jesus in order to be an apostle?" It is my conviction that the answer is no. One does not have to have had a literal vision of Christ. However, they must have a unique vision, encounter, and revelation of Christ.

With Peter, there was a unique revelation of Christ. After he shared it with Jesus, Jesus said that this understanding did not come by way of natural means but by divine revelation. With that, Jesus gave him a different name and revealed to him his function. Notice that Jesus did not reveal His identity when Peter saw Jesus naturally, but He revealed it to Peter once he saw Jesus spiritually or by *revelation*. Jesus then says, "Upon this rock (this idea that Jesus is the Christ) I will build my church."

Apostles also have a unique vision of Christ historically, a unique vision of Him societally, locally, regionally, and globally. Hear me! Apostles do not just envision Christ in their local church. Apostles have a vision of Christ that is beyond the local church. Any individual who is only focused on their local church is not an apostle. Apostles see the need for Christ locally but also have a burden for Christ regionally and globally.

Every apostle in the Scriptures had a unique revelation of Christ. Paul said that what he preached did not come from man but through the revelation of Christ. Apostolic leaders, therefore, have different levels of revelation. All true apostles will be revelatory. If an individual does not have a scriptural as well as revelatory word, he or she is not an apostle.

6. Kingdom of God Establishmentarian

I have planted, Apollos watered; but God gave the increase. So then neither is he that planteth any thing, neither he that watereth; but God that giveth the increase. Now he that planteth and he that watereth are one: and every man shall receive his own reward according to his own labour. For we are labourers together with God: ye are God's husbandry, ye are God's building.
—1 Corinthians 3:6-9

Am I am not an apostle? am I not free? have I not seen Jesus Christ our Lord? are not ye my work in the Lord? If I be not an apostle unto others, yet doubtless I am to you: for the seal of mine apostleship are ye in the Lord.
—1 Corinthians 9:1-2

Friends, let us not forget our working definition of an apostle. An apostle is a fully empowered and authorized ambassador sent by and on behalf of Christ to go into foreign territories where Christ is not known or not known well, to establish or reestablish Kingdom of God government, civilization, and culture. Once the foundation has been solidified, the apostle and their apostolic team leave that territory to go and establish or reestablish Christ's government, civilization, and culture somewhere else.

In the above-mentioned Scriptures, one of Paul's claims for being an apostle was not that he planted a church, but rather that he planted or established Kingdom of God government, civilization, and culture. The establishing of a church is just a byproduct of the laying down of a Kingdom of God foundation. However, a business could be the byproduct of the laying down of a Kingdom of God foundation. So could an invention, a school, and even new legislation be the byproduct of the laying down of a Kingdom of God foundation.

Remember, Ephesians 2:19-20 reminds us that the Church is built upon **the foundation of the apostles.** Here we see the emphasis is not so much on church planting but rather on foundation laying, that is, Kingdom of God establishment. An apostle is always thinking, always praying, "Thy kingdom come, Thy will be done in earth, as it is in heaven."

According to Scripture, if you have not established or re-established a Kingdom of God government, civilization, or culture, you are not an apostle. Yes, this may include church planting. However, just because you have planted or helped establish a church, it does not make you an apostle.

James, the half brother of Jesus, was an apostle, but from what we can surmise through Scripture and history, he never planted a church. But the Scriptures still claim him to be an apostle. One of the reasons for this is that he played an important role in establishing a church. This was the very first church, the church at Jerusalem. Subsequently, James became the very first official bishop (at that time, the term *bishop* was synonymous with *pastor*) of the church at Jerusalem.

Therefore, scripturally and historically, you must have either established or have been very instrumental in the establishment of a Kingdom of God government (*maybe church*), civilization, and culture to be deemed an apostle.

Let us now turn to the household of faith.

The Household of Faith: Two Rooms

*As we have therefore opportunity, let us do good unto all men,
especially unto them who are of the household of faith.*
—Galatians 6:10

Why is it that I do not specify that one must establish a church if they are indeed an apostle? Why is the claim for apostleship rather than one that establishes or re-establishes Kingdom of God government, civilization, or culture?

Usually, when we think of an apostle, we think of someone assigned to a local church or local churches. Maybe we think of someone who preaches every Sunday or Sabbath, or possibly someone who pastors other church pastors. All of this is true. However, the apostles who lead in the local church assembly are not the only apostles that exist.

Oftentimes, we think that Sundays, steeples, and praise teams are sacred, but weekdays, business meetings, and employment are secular. Friends, all of it is sacred! It all belongs to the Lord. That's why Psalm 24:1 declares, *"The earth is the LORD'S, and the fulness thereof; the world, and they that dwell therein."* There is no divide. Everything belongs to God ultimately, although everything does not belong to God intimately.

On the other hand, Satan owns nothing. Whatever system the devil intimately occupies, God has sent and is sending apostolic individuals to kick him out. Since God owns music and since the music industry does not always glorify God, go and kick the devil out. Since God owns the justice system, and since the justice system does not always glorify God, go and kick the devil out. Since God owns education and since the educational system does not always glorify God, go and kick the devil out. The devil does not even pay God rent for occupying territory that he does not own. He is a squatter, so go kick him out. That is what Christ commissions His apostles in Mark 16:15: *"Go ye into all the world . . ."* Go everywhere!

The household of faith is the Church, and we have seen that the Church is also the Bride of Christ. In this present age, there are two rooms in which the household of faith operates. Therefore, not every apostle will operate in the same room.

The Kitchen Apostle

The kitchen is one of the rooms in which the household of faith operates. It is in the kitchen that everyone in the household gets fed and has enough nutrition to be sustained through the week. The kitchen represents the local church assembly, where all the Body of Christ should gather. It is so sad that many claim to be a part of the household but never gather in the kitchen with other members for nourishment, fellowship, edification, and strength.

Sunday service is kitchen ministry. A sermon, a praise team, and a *"preach preacher"* are kitchen ministry too. See, like a pastor, *kitchen* apostles cook and serve the meals. Anything that has to do with the gathering of the saints is kitchen ministry, and so is anything that has to do with organized service.

Church planting is also kitchen ministry. If you claim to be an apostle in the kitchen (anything relating to temple ministry) and you have not established a church, helped to establish a church, or anything related to church or official ministry organization, according to Scripture, you are not an apostle.

In the ninth chapter of 1 Corinthians, the apostle Paul tells the church at Corinth that they are the seal of his apostleship. In other words, one of the proofs or markers that he was truly an apostle was the people (civilization) that were won for Christ.

However, let us pause for a moment and look at it more contextually. This was not just a new church that Paul established. This was a new church of new believers. Do not forget the context. Establishing a church of already saved and mature believers is not a sign of apostleship. The question should be, within this new church, how many of these individuals are new in Christ *and* how many people in this church have returned to Christ because of this church? New converts and repented backslidden saints in a newly established church are truly an apostolic marker.

There is nothing fundamentally apostolic about establishing a church by recruiting individuals who are already mature believers who have moved from another church. Yes, you need mature believers on the apostolic team who will help establish the church. However, witnessing to and preaching to already committed church believers is not evangelism. It is stealing.

There will also be believers, sheep, who will be scattered. These believers might not be attending a local church assembly. Yes, go after them. But if the church you established does not have a significant number of newly converted saints or repented backslidden saints, then the people who are there are not the seal of your apostleship. Remember the working definition of an apostle: "an apostle is a fully empowered and authorized ambassador sent by and on behalf of Christ to go into foreign territories where Christ is not known, or known well, to establish or reestablish Kingdom of God government, civilization, and culture. Once the foundation has been solidified, the apostle and his or her apostolic team leave that territory to go and establish or reestablish Christ's government, civilization, and culture somewhere else."

As an apostle, you do not plant in already established gardens. Apostles plant in already established weeds. Apostles plant where there has been an infestation of bugs, rodents, and critters. Apostles uproot deep-rooted principalities. Apostles toil on stubborn ground. Apostles plant in dark soil, in dark cities, in dark regions, in dark environments. Apostles do not try to find places where churches are already thriving to plant in. Apostles try to find territory where churches are dying or are nonexistent, and plant in that ground.

Let me reiterate this very important distinction. Apostles do not say, "Churches thrive in that city. I am going to plant a church there as well." That is not a sign of an apostle. On the contrary, apostles find the darkest environments and then say, "Let THERE be light!" True apostles look for new territory. Look at what the apostle Paul said: "*I have made it my aim to preach the gospel, not where Christ was named, lest I should build on another man's foundation*" (Romans 15:20).

As I mentioned before, the apostles in Scripture were foundation layers.

They laid the foundation of the first local churches. Today, there will be many apostles who are establishmentarians, just as there will also be apostles who are re-establishmentarians. These apostles will be challenged to reestablish the foundation of the Kingdom of God in churches and systems that have forsaken the foundation that was once laid. These apostles might lead a local church for a season to help facilitate revival. Some apostles will be sent to preach a particular biblical doctrine that is no longer taught prominently or well. These apostles dig up what was buried over time. We will expound on this later.

These *kitchen* apostles may not all be establishmentarians of churches. However, they will all be establishmentarians of church government as it relates to temple ministry. In other words, some apostles will establish fellowships, Christian organizations, networks, church planting networks, clergy coalitions, para-church ministries, and so on. Even if they have not established a local church, they have been used of God to establish a form of church government. These types of apostles have a desire and burden to resource the Body and bring the Body of Christ together in their community, city, region, state, country, or even the world.

There is a Caucasian sister in my city, Wilmington, North Carolina, who established One Christian Network. She established it to help unite the Body of Christ in Wilmington and to help resource them. I wonder if she has any clue that her work is apostolic, though I am not calling her an apostle. However, what she has done and is doing is definitely apostolic.

The Living Room Apostle

The second room in the household of faith is the living room. The living room symbolizes day-to-day operations and routine work. The difference with the kitchen ministry is this. While the kitchen ministry functions in the *religious* place, the living room ministry functions in the *marketplace*. The apostle in the kitchen serves in temple ministry. The apostle in the living room serves in template ministry. They pattern Monday through Friday in the workforce that which was pronounced on Sunday in the temple. The apostle in the kitchen primarily serves those who have gathered. The apostle in the living room primarily serves those who have been sent. One does his work in the sanctuary, whereas the other does his work in society.

The apostle who operates in the living room will not necessarily be a church planter. They might not ever preach a sermon. They might not ever have an official leadership role in a local church. But this apostle is establishing Kingdom of God government, culture, and civilization in the workforce.

Now, even if this apostle might not ever plant churches, they might very well plant businesses. They do not establish businesses for their own sake. They use it as a stepping stone to go into foreign territories where Christ is not known, or not known well. They may go in via education, politics, the beauty industry, the entertainment industry, the medical field, the media, to establish or reestablish Kingdom of God government, civilization, and culture. The living room apostle might be a game changer in science, grant-writing, the medical field, the technology industry, sales, the film industry, politics, and even the military. It all belongs to God!

One of the greatest examples of this is the late S. Truett Cathy, founder of—*drum roll, please*—Chick-fil-A. The purpose of this billion-dollar franchise was not just to make money or cook good chicken. Their website states that their corporate purpose is: "To glorify God by being a faithful steward of all that is entrusted to us. To have a positive influence on all who come in contact with Chick-fil-A."

Mr. Cathy was on assignment. His conviction for his establishment not to be open on Sundays so that people could rest and worship the Lord speaks to his intentionality to establish or reestablish Kingdom of God government, civilization, and culture in foreign territories where Christ is not known, or known well.

What is further apostolic fruit is franchising this establishment. There are over 3,000 Chick-fil-A locations all over the world. Let us not forget the second aspect of what apostles do. Once the foundation has been solidified, the apostle and their apostolic team leave that territory to go and establish or reestablish Christ's government, civilization, and culture somewhere else. That is what Cathy did when he began franchising. He took this Kingdom culture to other territories. Franchising can indeed be apostolic in principle. Now, God is being glorified in the restaurant industry.

Moreover, look at how other restaurants have mimicked Chick-fil-A. Everywhere I go, I see different restaurants having staff meet customers at their vehicles with iPads and with greater customer service. See, apostles are often mimicked. They are often copied. For reasons of my own, I did not make this a specific marker in the chapter. However, replication is truly apostolic fruit. Apostles will be mimicked by those who love them and by those who envy them. It comes with the territory.

Now, I am not saying that Mr. Cathy was or was not an apostle. What I am saying is that his life bore apostolic fruit. He was not a church planter. However, he was a planter or establishmentarian of Kingdom of God government, civilization, and culture. There are so many individuals who are establishing the government, culture, and civilization of God in the center of dark industries. They might not be apostles who lead in the temple, but they are apostles who are leading, pioneering, and shifting culture in society.

Take, for instance, NFL Hall of Famer and College Football Coach, Deion Sanders. Coach Sanders, a.k.a. Prime Time, may not preach on Sunday. He may not even be called Pastor Sanders at his local church. He might not ever be officially ordained. However, Coach Sanders is a fivefold ascension gift pastor. Oh yes, he is! He is not a pastor in the sanctuary. He is a pastor in society. His sheep are those college athletes who look to him for practical and spiritual guidance. There are even celebrities who have turned to Christ because of him.

To be honest, he probably has more influence in the world than any pastor of a local church. Although brother Deion does not carry the pastoral title, he bears the pastoral fruit.

So, within the fivefold ministry, some will be called to the sanctuary, while others will be called to society. If you think about it, the fivefold gift called, "evangelist" was originally called to society, not to the sanctuary. The very first evangelist that we see in Scripture, besides Jesus, was Philip. He was ministering in society, wherever the Lord called him to go, whether it was Samaria, the road to Gaza, or Azotus. However, today we *recognize* more evangelists in the sanctuary than we do in society.

Therefore, apostles will be Kingdom of God establishmentarians in either the sanctuary, society, or both.

So far, we have looked at six visible marks or signs of an apostle. Here is the seventh one.

7.   Master Builder/Architect

According to the grace of God which is given unto me, as a wise masterbuilder, I have laid the foundation, and another buildeth thereon. But let every man take heed how he buildeth thereupon.
—1 Corinthians 3:10

The apostle Paul states that God gave him the grace to be a wise master builder. This word *grace* in the text is the Greek word *charis*. It means supernatural ability. God gave Paul the supernatural ability to build wisely and masterfully. This wisdom to build a church so successfully did not come from a church planting conference; neither did it come from his natural intellect. This wisdom came supernaturally. It is the grace to build wisely that apostles carry. Some apostles have greater grace for building wisely than others. When I say greater, I do not mean value, but I mean in volume—greater in potency.

However, the grace to build wisely rests on all God-commissioned apostles.

Furthermore, Paul said this grace enabled him to be not only a wise builder, but a master builder. The Greek word for *master builder* is *architekton*, from where we get the word *architect*[18].

The ancient master builder existed for about 5,000 years. The master builder is a design-build professional. The Greeks gave the ancient master builder the name *architekton*, from which the Romans derived the Latin name, *architectus*. Both words literally mean master builder—denoting one responsible for both the design and construction of an edifice.

The traditional *architekton* is akin to the modern-day *architect*, but they are not synonymous. The traditional architect of a past era was someone who assumed overall responsibility for designing and constructing the edifice. They had to conceive the design, sketch it out, and then also build it out. They had to be present and work at the building site—work that included the organization of tradespeople and the supervision of workers. Their work was, in fact, an extension of the role of the craftsman.

So, in one person, the master builder was the one responsible for:

1. Design—encompassing deep artistic abilities; drawing skills; profound understanding of how people live and dwell; art/design knowledge for actual shaping, constructing, and all elements of the built environment (including buildings/parts of buildings, interiors, exterior landscapes, urban environments).

2. Construction—encompassing expert craftsmanship in the building arts; knowledge about how a beautiful building (or other environment) is built, as gained from actual construction experience; on-site project management (involving leadership, organizing/supervising workers, financial oversight, artistic discernment).

3. Building Site Authority—authority over on-site design/construction decisions; authority over all workers; unquestioned authority over the entire construction phase from start to finish.

So, the traditional architect, this master builder, was the designer, contractor, and general foreman all rolled into one. When Paul states that he is a wise master builder, he is saying that after God gave him the vision of the design for this church, he went about the actual construction of the foundation of this church, and he was the human authority over this church, even if someone else stepped in to build upon the foundation.

By the 1900s, the ancient concept of master builder was extinct. This has given way in our modern-day society to two individuals: 1) the architect, who is responsible for design *only*, but not skilled in building the edifice, and 2) the general contractor, who is responsible for construction *only*, but not skilled in design.

Apostles are the traditional *architekton* master builders. They not only design, but they also construct. Apostles are wise master builders. As wise master builders, apostles lay firm foundations. We will elaborate on foundation laying in a moment. However, if the foundation of something is not strong, whatever is erected upon that foundation will not last. Therefore, apostles plant churches that last. Apostles plant businesses that last. Apostles plant networks that last. I am not saying that what apostles build will last forever. Absolutely not. However, planting a church that only lasts for three years is not apostolic.

I am also not saying that apostles will not fail at times in their attempt to build. Apostles are human and are prone to error just like anyone else. Nevertheless, apostolicity is proven by what lasts, not by what begins. If one is always starting a church and closing a church, he or she is not an apostle. Elasticity confirms apostolicity. Apostles are wise in the building process.

8. Pioneers New Paths and New Territories/Trendsetter

Wherefore, holy brethren, partakers of the heavenly calling, consider
the Apostle and High Priest of our profession, Christ Jesus . . .
—Hebrews 3:1

The apostle Paul lets us know that Jesus the Christ is an apostle. Not just an apostle, Christ is THE Apostle. Jesus is the quintessential apostle. But how is Jesus an apostle? Well, the answer is revealed in Paul's declaration, *"Christ is the Apostle of our profession."* What do we profess? We profess that we are saved through faith in the name of Jesus. We profess that we no longer need a priest to sacrifice an animal once a year for our sins because Jesus sacrificed Himself once for all. We profess that God's people are not just those of Jewish descent, but they are anyone who repents and confesses Him as Lord and Savior.

In context, this Christian profession was something new. It was something the Jews and the Gentiles had never heard of. It was a new era. When Paul claims that Jesus is the apostle of our profession, he is saying that Jesus is the Pioneer of our Faith because that is what an apostle is—a pioneer. Apostles blaze the trail for others to walk through. Apostles are spearheads. Apostles do things that have either never been done or have never been done in their industry, region, era, or organization. Again, this is why true apostles are often mimicked both by people who love them and those who envy them.

The pioneering grace of apostles favors them with both innovation and excavation. With innovation, they think of new ideas, new strategies, new systems, and new ways of doing old things. With excavation, they plow into new territory. They might lead the church (local, regional, church at large, etc.) into a new technology territory that the church has never witnessed before. In business, they might merge two industry fields together that their business (or business field) has never encountered. This grace of innovation and excavation gives them a grace for replication. Many begin to replicate what the apostle has pioneered. This is why apostles lead leaders. We will discuss this soon. However, since the apostle has new favor, new concepts, and new territory that others have not seen, leaders will flock to them asking the questions, "How?" and "Why?"

This is the grace that rests on authentic apostles. They do not follow trends; they are the godly trendsetters. A great example of this was the German theologian Martin Luther[19]. In the 1500s, many scholars began to question the doctrine and practices of the Roman Catholic Church, Martin Luther being one of them. Martin Luther was very troubled by the corruption and the extravagant living of the pope and the clergy. He initially started to question their practices and doctrine of the sale of indulgences.

This doctrine, in part, was that individuals would have to pay them money to purchase the forgiveness of sins. Luther also detested the idea that we are saved by works, and stressed that we are saved by grace through faith in Christ Jesus alone. Martin Luther posted his grievances, known as the ninety-five theses, on the door of the church of Wittenberg to bring reformation to the Roman Catholic Church. As a consequence, he was labeled a heretic and excommunicated from the Roman Catholic Church.

As a consequence, the Protestant Church (PROTESTant) was birthed. Any Christian Church that is not Roman Catholic (or Orthodox) and believes the justification of sinners by grace through faith alone, the priesthood of all believers, and the Bible as the sole authority of the truth (*sola scriptura*) is a part of the Protestant Church. That includes the majority of churches in America.

Martin Luther was a major pioneer. What about John Wesley, the founder of the Methodist Church? What about our sister Aimee Semple McPherson, the founder of The Foursquare International Church? These are indeed apostolic mothers and fathers.

9. Foundation Layers/Restorers

> *Now therefore ye are no more strangers and foreigners, but fellow*
> *citizens with the saints, and of the household of God, and are built*
> *upon the foundation of the apostles and prophets, Jesus Christ Himself*
> *being the chief corner stone . . .*
> **—Ephesians 2:19-20**

Paul declares that the Church is built upon the foundation of the apostles and prophets. The Greek word *themelios* is the word that Paul uses for *foundation*. This word comprises the Greek words *lithos* and *tithemi*. The word *lithos* means *stone*. The word *tithemi* means *to lay something down*. *Themelios*, therefore, means *to lay something down in stone*, or better, *an understructure that is set in stone*. This under-structure, this foundation, is stable, strong, and not easily moved. Does this remind you of the wise master-builder trait?

Apostles lay the organizational foundation, the doctrinal foun-dation, the ethical foundation, and the cultural foundation. The original apostles laid the foundation of the Church. However, mod-ern-day apostles lay the foundation of the local church (microcosm) and may relay the foundation of the Church (macrocosm) by re-forming it after the enemy has attempted to confiscate it. Let me ex-plain further. The foundation of the Church at large was already laid by the early apostles. That foundation cannot be changed. However, there are certain truths in the Body of Christ that have been lost or buried through corruption, oversight, or neglect. It could be the foundational truth about prayer, discipleship, or even the truth in regard to providing for the poor.

Modern-day apostles will restore foundations that the enemy has attempted to erode. That is what Martin Luther did. The foundation that was already laid by the original Apostles seems to have been corrupted by the Roman Catholic Church, so he was commissioned to re-lay the foundation.

Again, different revelations and convictions may come to different apostles within the Body. One apostle might have a core message within their apostolic ministry about prayer; to another, it might be about giving to the poor. So apostles can go into territory where God's Name is known but where some of His foundational principles have been hijacked. They then re-lay the original foundation.

If they are planting a local church, they lay the foundation of the local church based upon the foundation laid for the Church at large by the original Apostles. However, that local church's foundation might be about focusing on children's ministry or becoming more outreach-based than another local church. This is because the apostle laid a particular foundation that might differ from another's foundation. Nevertheless, although particular local church foundations may differ, the substratum of all those churches should be the same, and that is "Jesus Christ is Lord." He is the Rock on which the Church is built.

An individual who does not lay a biblical foundation or even care about a biblical foundation, the tenets of our faith, is not an apostle. The teaching of God's Word is foundational. Prayer is a foundation. Order and organization are a foundation. On the other hand, praise breaks are good but are not foundational. Having great music is a huge asset, but it is not foundational. The foundation is what the Church is built on. If the local church is not built or does not remain on a godly foundation, we should not expect such a church to prevail over time.

Again, apostles are foundation layers but not necessarily foundation stayers. Once the foundation is laid, the apostle will either leave that assignment to start a new one or continue the assignment, parallel to starting a new assignment. Not understanding this basic truth, many congregations frustrate apostles by trying to hold them down as pastors. You will always be an apostle assassin when you do not understand and uphold an apostle's assignment.

In the Book of Genesis, we find the nature of God to be truly apostolic. Watch what God does. Watch how He builds. Watch how

He creates the world progressively in stages. Although He can create everything at once, He chooses to layer it in stages, teaching us how to be wise master builders.

Also, notice that when God creates, He does not create the vegetation before He creates the land. If He did, where would the vegetation go? He does not create the land animals before He creates the vegetation. If He did, what would they eat? He does not create the birds before He creates the firmament (sky). If He did, where would they survive and thrive? God takes His time and builds layer upon layer of foundation. That is apostolic!

But watch this. After God creates the foundation progressively in stages, on the sixth day, He creates mankind. And then He turns what He has built over to mankind and expects mankind to build upon that foundation. That is what apostles do! They lay the foundation and turn it over to another to continue building upon. This leads us to our next apostolic marker.

10. **Transitory**

And when it was day, he departed and went into a desert place: and the people sought him, and came unto him, and stayed him, that he should not depart from them. And he said unto them, I must preach the kingdom of God to other cities also: for therefore am I sent.
—Luke 4:42-43

Apostles are transitory, on the move all the time. Please remember, historically, what an apostle was at least 300 years before Jesus Christ came to earth. The apostle's job was to replicate the emperor's civilization, government, and culture in other areas and regions populated by barbarians. Once this difficult and dangerous task was completed, the apostle would travel to another region and do it again.

This is the ministry of an apostle. Apostles do not stay still. Luke 4:42-43 is truly an apostolic text. The people are trying to keep Jesus all to themselves—understandably so. They love Jesus. They have been blessed by Jesus. They feel safe with Jesus. However, Jesus says something that is loaded with apostolic revelation. He says, *"I must preach the kingdom of God to other cities also: for therefore I am sent."*

The Greek word for *sent* here is *apostellō*. *Apostellō* is the verb from which *apóstolos* is derived. In other words, Jesus is saying, "I cannot stay here with you. I must preach the kingdom of God in other cities because that is why I am an Apostle!" Do you see? He is sharing with us that apostles are not stationary; they are mobile.

Apostles go from this church to that church, from this region to the next region, for the purpose of breaking new ground. Selfish churches never benefit from the grace of an apostle. Trying to limit an apostle to only a pastoral grace will not just frustrate the apostle but will also stifle the anointing that is on their life. Apostles are not your traditional pastors.

Apostles are transitory. True bishops are transitory, too. They are always on the move, checking on different churches, encouraging senior leaders. All true bishops are apostolic in function, yet not all bishops are fivefold apostles. So, while the pastoral grace is a staying grace, the apostolic grace is a transitory one.

II. Leader of Leaders

Other senior leaders seem to flock to apostles. An apostle is an individual from whom other leaders desire to glean. Apostles are parents of pastors, spiritually speaking. Remember, we stated that apostles are foundation layers. Yet, they are leaders of leaders. In other words, apostles do both the groundwork and the roof-work.

With their groundwork, they lay the foundation. With their roof-work, they provide oversight and leadership to senior leaders or even the church covering. In this way, apostles provide both foundation and shelter.

What about the "Living Room Apostles" that some call Marketplace Apostles? These might be mentors to business owners, political leaders, or even entertainers.

When we say that an apostle is a leader of leaders, we have a two-fold meaning. They lead leaders as well as they lead in leading (the quintessential leader). They are a mature example of what a leader looks like, which brings us to our next apostolic marker.

12. **Mature**

It really grieves me that there are so many who claim to be apostles but are still immature. When we look at some social media posts and observe preaching content and lifestyle choices, how many of these individuals are mature? Many who claim apostleship are not even mature human beings. Sad, but unfortunately true. Apostleship is not a call to vestments, thrones, prominence, loftiness, or people tithing to you. No, this is a call to maturity. Apostleship does not look like an ascension in the Kingdom. Apostleship is a death sentence! This is why the gift apostle is very different.

---

*. . . unto every one of us is given grace according to the measure of the gift of Christ. Wherefore he saith, When he ascended up on high, he led captivity captive, **and gave gifts unto men**. (Now that he ascended, what is it but that he also descended first into the lower parts of the earth? He that descended is the same also that ascended up far above all heavens, that he might fill all things. **And he gave some, apostles**; and some, prophets; and some, evangelists; and some, pastors and teachers . . .*
—Ephesians 4:7-11

---

*But the Lord said unto him, Go thy way: for he is a chosen vessel unto me, **to bear my name before the Gentiles**, and kings, and the children of Israel: for I will shew him, how great things he must suffer for my name's sake.*
—Acts 9:15-16

As they ministered to the Lord, and fasted, the Holy Ghost said, Separate me Barnabas and Saul for the work whereunto I have called them. And when they had fasted and prayed, and laid their hands on them, they sent them away . . .
—Acts 13:2-3

The Scriptures let us know that Christ gave gifts to mankind. What are these gifts? According to Ephesians 4, the gifts are apostles, prophets, evangelists, pastors, and teachers. When Paul says that Christ gave *some*, what is He referring to? *Some* refers to the people that Christ gave the gifts to. In other words, Christ gave the gift of *apostle* to *some* people. He gave the gift of *prophet* to *some* people.

The point is this: the *apostle* in Ephesians 4:11 is not called an office. It is actually called a spiritual gift that comes from Christ. However, the office of *apostle* must be conferred by His Body. You can have the gift of *apostle* (or apostolic gift), but not yet have the fruit of an apostle. In the Economy of God, His human representatives confer an office upon another, not based upon their gift, but based upon their fruit. The gift of the tree is the seed of the tree, but the office or title of the tree is conferred by the fruit it bears.

One of the reasons that Jesus rebukes the fig tree in Matthew chapter 21 is that the fig tree has fig seed and fig leaves, but it does not have fig fruit. A tree that is not *mature* never produces fruit. You may have the seed (gift), but if you do not have the fruit, it is because you are not mature enough to exemplify the title (office). Just because you prophesy does not mean that you are a prophet. Just because you give great advice does not make you a pastor.

This is one of the reasons why so many who possess true apostolic seed (the gift of apostle) claim an office before they are ready. They might have had a true apostolic call. However, the initial call of God is not to proclaim, but rather to prepare. This is why many immature *prophets* will see a gift in an individual and prophesy an office on them way before its season.

Paul's apostolic call, for instance, was at the very same time as his conversion call. When Christ called Saul, the first aspect of his call was that he would bear Christ's Name to the Gentiles. This was huge. No one at this time had preached the Gospel to the Gentiles. Paul would be a *pioneer* to the Gentiles, an apostle to them. That calling came from Christ. However, although Christ Himself indicated to Paul that his apostolic ministry was primarily to the Gentiles, he did not walk in that apostolic grace until fourteen to seventeen years later.

In the intervening years, he walked as a disciple before he stepped into the role of an apostle. He was a sat-one (disciple) before he was a sent-one (apostle). It was not until the prophets and teachers laid hands on him and authorized him in Acts chapter 13, fourteen to seventeen years after Jesus called him, that he walked in the office of apostle, although he already had the gift of apostle.

Why did it take Paul so long? Paul still had to mature. Before Saul's call, he was arresting and murdering Christians. Before Saul's call, he was one of the most zealous of Jews. After his conversion, with all that he had done, with all the violence that he was known for doing, with all that he thought was right, it took some time for him to mature and for others to trust him.

Individuals who truly have the gift of apostle must take their time. God desires you to become something before you are called something. We confer the office not because of apostolic gift (charisma), but because of apostolic fruit (character). This should be true in all aspects of official church leadership.

One of the truest signs that an office should be conferred upon another is not giftedness, but rather maturity. If there is anyone who claims to be an apostle but they are not mature, they are not an apostle.

13. **Maternal and Paternal in Relationship**

---

*Am I not an apostle? am I not free? have I not seen Jesus Christ our Lord? are not ye my work in the Lord? **If I be not an apostle unto others, yet doubtless I am to you: for the seal of mine apostleship are ye in the Lord.***
— 1 Corinthians 9:1-2

True ascension gift apostles will be both maternal and paternal in their functions. Again, this is not about physical gender. We are talking spiritually. Birthing is a maternal function. These apostles may birth a church or other entities (those kitchen apostles) and/or birth pastors assigned to churches. Apostles may also father other leaders, whether or not they came initially from their ministry.

If an individual is a father to other senior leaders but has not birthed a church or a network, that individual may simply be serving as a bishop (although the function of a bishop is apostolic). Moreover, just because someone seems maternal by way of initiating "so-called" churches, or even fellowships and networks, that does not make them a legitimate apostle. You see, an ascension gift apostle will be both maternal and paternal. As Paul was to the churches that he birthed, you are particularly an apostle to those you brought forth.

14. **Swiss Army Knife: Operates in All Fivefold Offices**

Another undeniable mark of an apostle is their ability—by grace—to function in all ascension gifts listed in Ephesians 4: Apostle, Prophet, Evangelist, Pastor, and Teacher. This is not about collecting titles or hoarding positions; it is about the necessity of the pioneering call. When you are pioneering and there is no infrastructure, no trained team, and no visible support system, the apostle has to be graced to do everything until others can join the work.

My pastor brought Daniel Boone, the legendary American frontiersman, to my attention. Boone did not ride into a ready-made city—he entered raw, untamed wilderness. There was no courthouse, no sheriff's office, no schoolhouse, and no paved road. If a settlement was to survive, Boone often had to be the sheriff, be the mayor, be the road crew, and even be the schoolteacher. He did not assume these roles for the sake of control or recognition—he did it because there was no one else yet to do them. This is the role of a pioneer. This is the reality of an apostle. When they step into new territory, they are the first settler, the lawman, the builder, and the teacher all in one.

This truth is embedded in the ancient Greek *apóstolos*. In the days before Christ, the *apóstolos* was sent by the emperor to establish a colony in foreign territory. Upon arrival, the admiral could not outsource leadership—he was the leadership. Yes, he had a team, but he still oversaw the building of roads, the training of locals, the enforcement of laws, and the establishment of the empire's culture. When Jesus called His sent ones "apostles," His listeners understood immediately: they were being sent into spiritual "uncivilized territory" to do whatever was necessary to reveal the Kingdom there.

Biblically, the apostle Paul models this grace with striking clarity. As an apostle, he planted works where Christ had not been named, laying foundations others would build upon (Romans 15:20). As a prophet, he foretold events like the famine in Acts 11 and the shipwreck in Acts 27, offering divine strategy in crisis. As an evangelist, he preached in hostile cities until entire communities were stirred and souls were saved. As a pastor, he wrote with the heart of a shepherd—pleading, correcting, and rejoicing over his spiritual children. As a teacher, he penned letters that still shape Christian doctrine today.

Peter carried this same grace: pioneering as an apostle, prophesying judgment as a prophet in Acts 5, preaching thousands into the Kingdom at Pentecost, shepherding persecuted believers, and teaching practical holiness in his letters. And then there is Jesus—the perfect pattern and our Chief Apostle (Hebrews 3:1)—who flawlessly embodied all fivefold offices, proving that true apostolic grace can shift fluidly into whatever role the mission demands.

This is why I liken these pioneering apostles to a Swiss Army knife. The Swiss Army knife is not the perfect tool for every job—it is the necessary tool when you have only one instrument to do whatever is required. One day, the apostle is preaching the gospel (the "blade"), the next they are counseling a weary leader (the "scissors"), then training a team (the "screwdriver"), then casting prophetic vision (the "compass"). They have just enough of each tool to keep the mission alive until the foundation has been laid with the arrival of specialized help.

For those Living Room Apostles (Marketplace Apostles), the fivefold function takes on unique and often unconventional forms, yet the grace behind it is the same. Their pulpit may be a boardroom, their congregation a team of employees, and their mission field an industry or city economy. The Kingdom flows through their leadership in ways that may not look "churchy" on the surface, but the apostolic DNA is there.

As prophets, they are the visionaries who can see the unseen. They discern industry shifts, cultural trends, and emerging opportunities long before they are visible to the masses. Like Agabus in Acts 11, they can sense what is coming and prepare for it before others even notice the signs.

As evangelists, they become the chief recruiters, marketers, and brand ambassadors for their vision. They do not just sell a product—they win people to a cause. They know how to tell the story of their mission in a way that draws investors, partners, customers, and collaborators into the fold.

As pastors, they shepherd their staff and teams. They watch over morale, protect company culture, and mediate conflicts. They see their people not as cogs in a machine but as souls with dreams, burdens, and families.

As teachers, they invest in the growth and development of those they lead. They pass on skills, strategies, and mindsets that ensure the mission can continue without them. They create training systems, mentorship pipelines, and resource materials that multiply leaders.

And as apostles, they chart the course. They establish new territory, define the mission's values, and secure the strategic partnerships that allow the work to scale. They think in terms of legacy—what must be in place so that, even after they leave, the culture and the mission remain intact?

Let me give you two pictures.

When Marcus received the call to start a faith-based coffee roasting company, he had no investors, no storefront, and no staff—just a word from God. From day one, Marcus was an apostle, building according to mission and securing territory. Soon, he was used as the prophet, sensing an industry shift toward ethically sourced, small-batch coffee before the trend exploded. He then showed forth the evangelist, sharing his story and winning customers one bag at a time. As a pastor, he cared for his team, praying with them and guiding them through challenges. And as a teacher, he trained staff not only in coffee skills but in life skills. Two years later, the company was thriving, and Marcus could pass specialized roles to others—but in those early days, he walked heavily in all five graces, because he was laying the foundation.

Now, all successful entrepreneurs operate in this manner. However, this does not mean that he or she is an apostle. What it does mean is that if he or she is filled with the Holy Spirit, he or she is walking in apostolic grace. The grace is for the entire Body of Christ. The gift or office is for "some."

Let me give you another story.

From the first day that Pastor Alicia landed in Chicago to establish a church, she walked as an apostle—walking neighborhoods, choosing meeting spaces, and defining the vision. She walked as a prophet, discerning strongholds, declaring God's promises over the region, speaking prophetically to those she encountered. She walked as an evangelist, sharing the gospel at parks, community events, and grocery store aisles. As a pastor, she cared for the first handful of members like family, visiting them in sickness and helping them through crises. As a teacher, she laid biblical foundations in living room Bible studies. Two years later, the church had a worship team, children's ministry, and trained leaders—but the culture had been set in those first months when she carried the whole load herself. Three years after that, she appointed a leadership team in Chicago and established another ministry in Detroit.

Apostles walk strong prophetically, evangelistically, pastorally, and didactically. Depending on the season, the terrain, and the need, the prominence of each grace will fluctuate.

Whether in a storefront church or a start-up business, the apostle is God's all-terrain instrument—versatile, adaptable, and graced to be whatever the moment demands. Like Daniel Boone riding into the wilderness with only what he could carry, apostles arrive in new territory not with luxury, but with the versatility to survive, build, and establish. And when the work is stable, they gladly hand the tools to others, fold up the Swiss Army knife, and ride on to the next frontier. That is the apostolic way.

This brings us to the crucial question: How do we authenticate apostolicity?

06

TESTING APOSTOLIC CLAIMS

We are living in an age when anyone can claim to be anything with the click of a "post" button. Apostolic titles are being thrown around like business cards at a networking event. The danger? Without discernment, the Body of Christ becomes vulnerable to smooth talkers, false builders, and charismatic personalities who sound good but carry no true apostolic grace.

The early church understood something we have almost forgotten: apostles are not self-appointed. They are God-sent and Church-recognized. Without a way to test claims, the Church opens herself to infiltration—not just from error, but from spiritual sabotage.

WHY TESTING MATTERS

A false apostle is not always an obvious wolf. Many start off sounding right, quoting Scripture, and drawing crowds. But somewhere along the line, their message shifts. Instead of building the Kingdom, they build their kingdom. Instead of serving Christ's mission, they serve their own ambition. Before long, the people following them find themselves far from sound doctrine—and even further from Christ.

We have seen churches split in half, relationships destroyed, and communities fractured because of unchecked "apostolic" claims. These self-appointed leaders may pull people into personality cults, set up competing visions, and even put believers against each other. Testing claims is not about suspicion—it is about protection. It safeguards unity, preserves sound doctrine, and shields the credibility of true apostles who labor with integrity.

And let us be clear: without discernment, scandals are inevitable. Scripture warns us that judgment begins at the house of God (1 Peter 4:17). When leaders are not tested, moral and doctrinal compromise creeps in. History is full of stories of unchecked leaders who ended up in financial corruption, sexual immorality, or spiritual abuse. Testing is God's safeguard to keep His Church pure.

BIBLICAL MANDATE TO TEST APOSTLESHIP

The Ephesian Church (Revelation 2:2) is commended by Jesus for testing those who claimed to be apostles and finding them false. That means there was a standard, and they had the courage to apply it. They were not swayed by charisma—they were anchored in truth.

The Bereans (Acts 17:10-11) show us the blueprint: they examined the scriptures daily to see if even Paul's words were true. Think about that—they did not give Paul a free pass just because of his reputation or his title. They made sure the message matched the Book.

Paul himself warned the Galatians (Galatians 1:6-9) that anyone—even an angel—preaching a different gospel should be rejected. Truth does not bend for titles, visions, or spiritual claims.

Jesus told us in Matthew 7:15-20 to look at the fruit. That is not just a metaphor for results—it is the sum of a person's character, doctrine, and long-term influence. Bad trees can only produce bad fruit, and time will expose it.

Paul, in defending his own apostleship (2 Corinthians 12:12), pointed to the "signs of a true apostle"—not only teaching and integrity, but the supernatural witness of the Holy Spirit confirming his ministry.

THE CHURCH'S ROLE IN TESTING

Testing apostleship is not a private opinion—it is a corporate responsibility.

Councils and Ecclesiastical Oversight

Historically, church councils have played a pivotal role in affirming and regulating apostolic claims. These gatherings of church leaders provide a forum for discussing and discerning matters of doctrine, practice, and leadership. Ecumenical councils, such as Nicaea, Chalcedon, and others, have been instrumental in addressing contentious issues, establishing orthodox Christian beliefs, and refuting heretical teachings.

In the context of affirming apostolic credentials, councils can evaluate claims through structured debate and communal wisdom. Drawing on the collective insights of credible spiritual and theological leaders, this ecclesiastical oversight ensures that claims are not based on individual charisma or untested revelations but are instead rooted in the broader historical and theological framework of the Church.

We need council-level wisdom—a gathering of tested leaders who can discern with both spiritual and scriptural authority.

Church Community Discernment

Church community discernment is another critical component in the process of affirming apostolic credentials. The Church community, as a collective body of believers, actively participates in evaluating the validity of claims through prayer, discussion, and reflection.

Engaging the wider church community fosters transparency and accountability, ensuring that decisions are not made in isolation but reflect the shared values and beliefs of the congregation. Through this process, the Church can discern spiritual authenticity, assess the fruit of a leader's ministry, and confirm that they conform to biblical and doctrinal standards.

Theological Education

Theological training and education also play a crucial role in preparing emerging apostles. Seminaries and theological institutions can provide rigorous academic and spiritual formation, equipping individuals with the knowledge, skills, and ethical grounding necessary for effective ministry.

By emphasizing sound doctrine, historical theology, and ethical leadership, these educational structures can help ensure that future leaders are well-prepared to navigate complex spiritual, societal, and ecclesiastical challenges. Continuous theological education also supports ongoing formation, enabling current leaders to respond adeptly to new issues in ministry.

Formal theological education is helpful but not a ticket to apostleship. Some of the greatest apostles in history never set foot in a seminary, yet they were students of the Word for life. However, anyone unwilling to keep learning—anyone who refuses to grow deeper in the Scriptures—should never be affirmed. An unteachable spirit is a disqualifier.

Spiritual Accountability

Mentorship and spiritual oversight contribute significantly to the process of affirming apostolicity. Experienced leaders within the Church provide guidance, mentorship, and oversight, supporting emerging apostles in their spiritual and ministerial development. This relational aspect encourages accountability, character formation, and adherence to the core tenets of the faith.

Mentorship allows for the transfer of practical wisdom and the cultivation of spiritual maturity, key components for those seeking to take on apostolic responsibilities.

Lone rangers may make great movie heroes, but they make dangerous spiritual leaders. True apostles walk under authority, receive correction, and welcome accountability.

A FRAMEWORK FOR TESTING APOSTOLIC CLAIMS

If the early church tested apostles, so must we. A sound process will examine:

1. **Biblical Alignment** – Do their teachings and actions match the Word? Do they walk in the fruit of the Spirit?

2. **Theological and Historical Understanding** – Are they sound in doctrine and rooted in the faith once delivered to the saints? Do they teach what the original Twelve Apostles taught? Are they committed to the foundations of the Christian faith

as traditionally understood and interpreted by mainstream Christianity?

3. **Character and Integrity** – Is their life above reproach? Are they accountable?

4. **Church Community Recognition** – Do seasoned leaders affirm their call? Is there long-term fruit from their ministry?

5. **Divine Calling and Gifting** – Is there a clear, confirmed apostolic call with evidence of apostolic grace?

6. **Engagement with the Wider Body** – Do they have the willingness and ability to interact and form constructive relationships with the broader Christian community? Are they contributing positively to the unity and mission of the Church as a whole?

This is not about legalism—it is about life and death for the mission. A false apostle can poison a movement. A true one can spark revival.

GUARDING THE GATE

In a world of titles without tests, the Church must guard the gate. We do not test individuals to shame them; we test them to protect the sheep, honor the calling, and preserve the credibility of the office. The goal is not suspicion—it is authenticity.

If we do the hard work of discernment now, we will reap the peace, unity, and power that comes from having leaders truly sent by God. As Jesus said, "You will know them by their fruit." Let us make sure the fruit is good, the roots are deep, and the calling is real.

By adhering to this thorough evaluation process, the Body of Christ can effectively discern and uphold true apostolic leadership. This ensures that those who claim such a mantle are equipped and called to guide others as God's chosen vessels.

THE APOSTOLIC ASSESSMENT

Based on Scripture and others who have shared deep studies on the contemporary apostolic, I can offer this system, "The Apostolic Assessment." I believe that this tool will be helpful in authenticating apostolicity.

The Apostolic Assessment comprises two parts. Part One has been systematized to validate true apostolic claims with greater accuracy. Part Two has been constructed to more prominently detect false apostolicity. Completing Part One will give one enough evidence to deem the apostolicity of the claimant as indeed authentic. Part Two further undergirds the answers that Part One provides.

Regarding Part One, eight out of ten questions should be answered "Yes" to help solidify one's apostolic claim. Answering these questions will also help to prove whether someone is a false apostle or one who is not mature enough for the office of apostle to be conferred.

As it relates to Part Two, if the claimant has at least two to three questions answered "Yes," he or she is probably a False Apostle.

Both sections of this assessment are complementary.

The Apostolic Assessment (Part 1)   Y   N

1. Have I (they) established churches, businesses, ministries, organizations, or even inventions that last?

2. Do senior leaders naturally look to me (them) for guidance?

3. Do other seasoned leaders see me (them) as an apostle without me (them) having to announce it for myself (themselves)?

4. Am I (are they) a trendsetter and a trailblazer?

5. Have I (they) established churches with new converts or with individuals who returned to Christ because of my (their) ministry?

6. Do I (they) have a track record of walking in the supernatural, both in signs and wonders?

7. Does God give me (them) access to new territory and success that others seem not to be able to gain access to, for the sake of reforming systems and liberating people groups?

8. Am I (are they) transitory—always working on different projects, different assignments, and possibly doing so in different places?

9. Is there a truth of the Scriptures that the Lord has used me (them) to restore in some major segment of the Body of Christ?

10. Do I (they) operate in all fivefold ministry gifts?

The Apostolic Assessment (Part 2)   Y   N

1. Am I (are they) immature?
2. Do I (they) keep starting and stopping churches, businesses, organizations, or ministries?
3. Do I (they) have a history of canceling service or quitting their assignment when things get challenging?
4. Is my (their) preaching and teaching superficial?
5. Does my (their) revelation of Christ and the things of God go against the Scriptures and our fathers of The Faith?
6. Am I (are they) prideful?
7. Am I (are they) manipulative?
8. Am I (are they) selfish?
9. Do I (they) seem to be ambitious for power, money, or prestige?
10. Do I (they) recruit/entice members from other church networks or organizations to join my (their) own?
11. Do I (they) seem to be a cowardly or a lazy leader?
12. Do I (they) seem to be an overbearing leader?
13. Do you discern that something is "off" regarding this individual?
14. Do I (they) reject human spiritual accountability?
15. Do I (they) only support my (their) own local church, business, or network?
16. Do I (they) bash other churches, businesses, or networks?

FINAL EXHORTATION

The call to apostleship is not a casual pursuit, nor is it a self-appointed badge of honor. It is a sacred commission that carries the weight of heaven's authority and the burden of advancing the Kingdom of God against the gates of hell. In every generation, the Lord raises up true apostles—men and women who will pioneer, build, govern, and guard the foundations of His Church. But in every generation, the enemy also sends counterfeits—voices that sound right but lead wrong, leaders that look anointed but lack God's approval.

This is why the testing of apostolic claims is not optional—it is obedience. To test is not to dishonor; it is to protect. To scrutinize is not to slander; it is to safeguard the faith once delivered to the saints. If the early church needed to "test those who say they are apostles and are not" (Revelation 2:2), how much more must we in an age where titles can be purchased, platforms can be manufactured, and charisma can be mistaken for calling?

The stakes are eternal. When false apostles go unchallenged, souls are lost, the Church is fractured, and the witness of Christ is tarnished. But when true apostles are recognized, affirmed, and released, the Church advances with clarity, unity, and power. Apostolic leaders are not raised up merely to be honored; they are sent to build, to battle, and to birth the purposes of God in their generation.

The responsibility now rests with us—the Body of Christ—to be discerning stewards of the apostolic mantle. We must hold every claim to the light of Scripture, measure every ministry by the fruit it bears, and submit every leader to the accountability of the community of faith. In doing so, we do not quench the Spirit—we protect the move of the Spirit from being hijacked by the flesh.

May we be like the Bereans, noble in our diligence to search the scriptures daily. May we be like the Ephesians, vigilant in testing those who claim to be sent ones. And may we be like Paul, whose life, labor, and love for the Church were living proof of his apostolic call.

The days ahead will demand more than gifted communicators and visionary planners. They will require builders with backbone, shepherds with scars, teachers with truth, evangelists with fire, prophets with purity, and apostles with unwavering loyalty to Jesus Christ. Let us rise to this moment with courage and conviction—recognizing the real, rejecting the counterfeit, and releasing those truly sent by God. For the harvest is great, the laborers are few, and the time is now.

And when history looks back on our generation, may it be said: *"They did not bow to titles, they did not chase trends, they contended for truth, and they kept the testimony of Jesus Christ untarnished in their day."*

NOTES

1   "Bishops, Elders, and Deacons," Christian-history.org, 2023, https://www.christian-history.org/bishops-elders-deacons.html.

2   Kuiper Douglas, "The History of the Office of Elder (5): Restored during the Reformation Era – the Standard Bearer Magazine by Reformed Free Publishing Association | RFPA," Rfpa.org, 2025, https://sb.rfpa.org/the-history-of-the-office-of-elder-5-restored-during-the-reformation-era/.

3   Warfield, B.B. Counterfeit Miracles. Charles Scribner's Sons, 1918.

4   MacArthur, John. Charismatic Chaos. Zondervan, 1992.

5   Irenaeus. Against Heresies. Translated by Alexander Roberts and W.H. Rambaut.

6   Tertullian. On the Soul and Against Marcion

7   The Didache. In The Apostolic Fathers, edited by Bart D. Ehrman.

8   Fee, Gordon D. God's Empowering Presence: The Holy Spirit in the Letters of Paul. Hendrickson Publishers, 1994.

9   Keener, Craig S. Gift and Giver: The Holy Spirit for Today. Baker Academic, 2001.

10   Storms, Sam. Practicing the Power: Welcoming the Gifts of the Holy Spirit in Your Life. Zondervan, 2017.

11   Hagin, Kenneth E. He Gave Gifts Unto Men: A Biblical Perspective of Apostles, Prophets, and Pastors. Tulsa, OK: Faith Library Publications, 1992.

12   "Ecclesia | Ancient Greek Assembly," Encyclopedia Britannica, n.d., https://www.britannica.com/topic/Ecclesia-ancient-Greek-assembly.

13   Myles Munroe, *Kingdom Principles* (Destiny Image Publishers, 2006).

14   Laurence J Cox, "How Old Were Jesus and His Disciples," Academia.edu, December 7, 2016, https://www.academia.edu/30309277/How_old_were_Jesus_and_his_disciples.

15   Rick Renner, *Apostles and Prophets* (Destiny Image Publishers, 2023).

16   Rick Renner, *Apostles and Prophets* (Destiny Image Publishers, 2023).

17   "Apostle - Apostolos (Greek Word Study) | Precept Austin," www.preceptaustin.org, n.d., https://www.preceptaustin.org/apostle_-_apostolos.

18   https://campbell-construction.com/masterbuilder/

19   https://www.britannica.com/biography/Martin-Luther